Mussoorie & Landour

The lyre tree, unique to Mussoorie, is
named for its remarkable shape. The
emblem of Woodstock School, this tree
is nearly as old as the school itself.

For our Parents

A rare picture of thatch-roofed Landour in the 1850s. During the monsoon, these leaked and were eventually replaced in the 1920s by the more practical but ugly galvanized tin roofs.

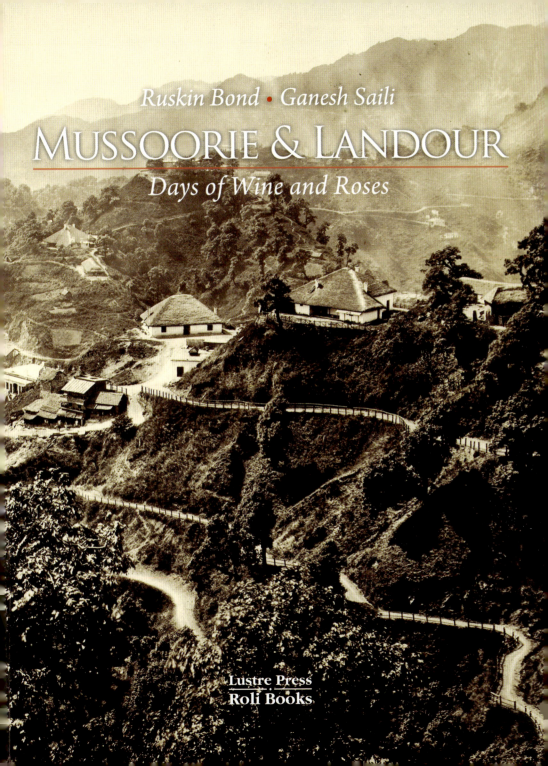

What is nostalgia but an attempt to preserve that which was good in the past? The past has served us well: let us serve it in this way.

– Ruskin Bond

Contents

The Mussoorie I Know	15
Birth of a Hill Station	25
Tales the Tombstones Tell	33
Tales of a Hill Station	41
The Schools Today	51
Up at the Top	60
Looking for John Lang	64
The Himalayan Club	70
A Mussoorie Miscellany	80

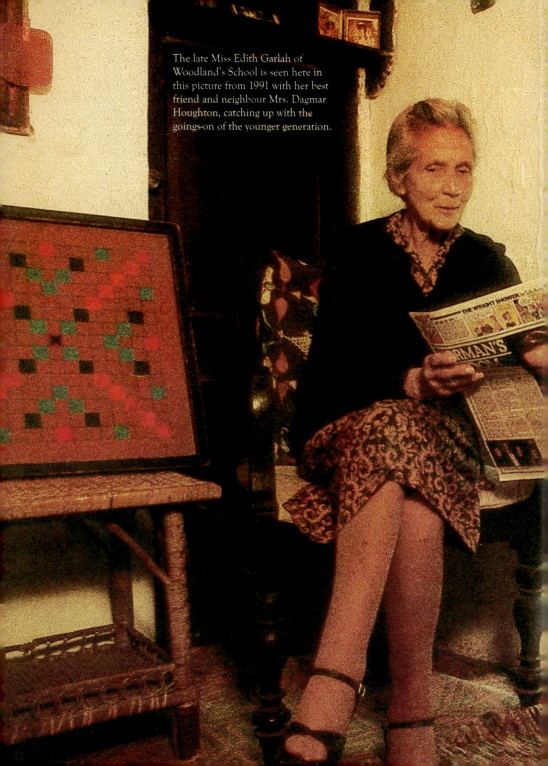

The late Miss Edith Garlah of Woodland's School is seen here in this picture from 1991 with her best friend and neighbour Mrs. Dagmar Houghton, catching up with the goings-on of the younger generation.

Bridges like this are tribute to early pioneers, such as the ironsmith Md. Rahim Baksh, the great-grandfather of Md. Khaliq, who built the one at Char Dukan. Khaliq's fine workshop on the ramp of Mullingar keeps many a vehicle chugging along long after its days should be over.

The sun lights up the world of Woodstock.

A 150-year-old view of Landour from St. Emillian's near the Himalaya Club reveals a plenitude of round-topped cypress, oak and rhododendrons, but few deodar trees.

Landour, the older part of Mussoorie, still remains unaffected by the explosion of new buildings seen in most other parts of Mussoorie.

The Mussoorie I Know

"Stand still for 10 minutes and they'll build a hotel on top of you," said one old-timer, gesturing toward the concrete jungle that had sprung up along Mussoorie's Mall, the traditional promenade. This hill station in northern India is now one long, ugly bazaar, but if you leave the mall and walk along some of the old lanes and by-ways, you will come across many of the old houses, most of them still bearing the names they were born with, back in the mid-19th century.

Mussoorie, like other hill resorts in India, came into existence in the 1820s or thereabouts, when the families of British colonials began making for the hills in order to escape the scorching heat of the plains. Small settlements grew into large "stations" and were soon vying with each other for the title of "queen of the hills". Mussoorie's name derives from the Mansur shrub (*Cororiana nepalensis*), common in the Himalayan foothills; but many of the house names derive from the native places of those who first built and lived in them. Today, the old houses and estates are owned by well-to-do Indians, many of whom follow the lifestyle of their former colonial rulers. In most cases, the old names have been retained.

Take, for instance, the Mullingar. This is not one of the better-preserved buildings, having been under litigation for some years, but it was a fine mansion once, and has the distinction of being Mussoorie's oldest building. It was the home of an Irishman, Captain Young, who commanded the first Gurkha battalion when in its infancy. As you have probably guessed, he came from Mullingar in old Ireland and it was to Ireland that he finally returned when he gave up his sword and saddle. There is a story that on moonlit nights a ghostly rider can be seen on the Mullingar flat, and that this is Captain Young revisiting old haunts.

There must have been a number of Irishmen settling and building in Mussoorie in those pioneering days, for there are houses with names such as Tipperary, Killarney, Shamrock Cottage, and Tara Hall. "The harp that once in Tara's Halls" must have sounded in Simla too, for there is also a Tara Hall in the old summer capital of India.

As everywhere, the Scots were great pioneers in Mussoorie too, and were quick to identify Himalayan hills and meadows with their own glens and braes. There are over a dozen house names prefixed with "glen" and close to where I live there is a Scottsburn, a Wolfsburn and a Redburn. A burn is a small stream, but there are none in the vicinity, so the name must have been given for purely sentimental reasons.

The English, of course, went in for castles – there's Connaught Castle, Grey Castle, Hampton Court and the Castle Hill, home for a time to the young Sikh prince, Dalip Singh, before he went to England to become a protege of Queen Victoria.

Sir Walter Scott must have been a very popular writer with the British in exile, for there are many houses in Mussoorie that echo his novels and romances – Kenilworth, Ivanhoe, Woodstock (now a well-known school), Rokeby, Waverly, The Monastery as also Abbotsford, named after Scott's own home.

Dickens' lovers must have felt frustrated because they could hardly name their houses Nicholas Nickleby or Martin Chuzzlewit; but one of them did come up with Bleak House, and bleak it is, even to this day.

Mussoorie did have a Dickens connection in the 1850s, when Charles Dickens was publishing his magazine *Household Words*. His correspondent in India was John Lang, a popular novelist and newspaper proprietor, who spent the last years of his life in Mussoorie. His diverting account of a typical Mussoorie "Season", called "The Himalaya Club", appeared in *Household Words* in the issue of 21 March 1857. Recently I was able to obtain a copy from the British Museum and it appears here for the first time since its original publications.

I haven't been able to locate the house in which Lang lived, but from a description of his it may have been White Park Forest, now practically a ruin. The name is another puzzle, because of park and forest there is no trace. But

on looking up an old guide, I discovered that it had been named after its joint owners, Mr. White, Mr. Park, and Mr. Forest.

It is well over 60 years since a parson lived in The Parsonage, and its owner today is Victor Banerjee, the actor, who received an Academy Award nomination for his role in David Lean's *A Passage To India*. Victor doesn't mind his friends calling him the Vicar but he does value his privacy.

Another name that puzzled me for a time was that of the old Charleville Hotel, now an academy for young civil servants. Was it French in its origins? Most of the locals always referred to it as the "Charley-Billy" Hotel, which I thought was an obvious mispronunciation; but the laugh was really on me. According to the records, the original owner had two sons, Charley and Billy, and he had named the hotel after them.

Local residents have got fed up offering me lifts on the road to our hilltop bank. As they drive up the steep road to Landour in third (or is it fourth?) gear, they see me plodding along on foot and out of the goodness of their hearts stop and open the door for me. Although I hate to disappoint them, I close the door, thank them profusely, and insist that I am enjoying my walk. They don't believe me, naturally; but with a shrug, the driver gets into gear again and drives off, although sometimes they have difficulty getting started, the hill being very steep. As I don't wish to insult them by reaching the Bank first, I sit on the parapet wall and make encouraging sounds until they finally take off. Then I renew my leisurely walk up the hill, taking note of the fact that wild geraniums and periwinkles have begun to flower, and that the whistling thrushes are nesting under the culvert over which those very cars pass every day.

Most people, car drivers anyway, think I'm a little eccentric. So be it. I am probably eccentric. But having come to the Himalayan foothills over 25 years ago in order to enjoy walking among them, I am not about to stop now, just because everyone else has stopped walking. The hills are durable in their attractions, and my legs have proved durable too, so why should we not continue together as before?

The friends who walked beside me, like Ganesh who takes photographs, now have their cars or spacious vans, and seldom emerge from them unless it be to seek refreshment at some wayside teashop or cafe. When I invite them to walk a few metres with me, they complain of breathlessness or of twinges in their hinges and rents in their ligaments.

The castle of Castle Hill Estate in Landour as it was in the 1860s: the bazaar had just sprung up and the trees were in their infancy.

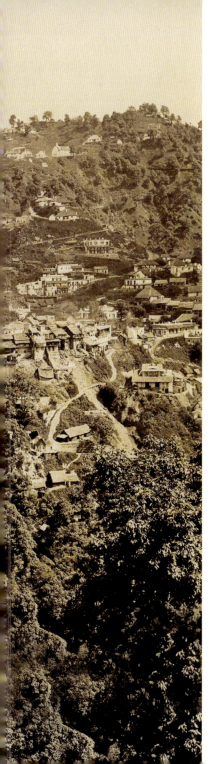

Now I'm no fitness freak. I don't jog either. If I did, I would almost certainly miss the latest wildflower to appear on the hillside, and I would not be able to stop a while and talk to other people on the road...villagers with their milk and vegetables, all-weather postmen, cheeky schoolchildren, inquisitive tourists...or to exchange greetings with cats, dogs, stray cows and runaway mules. Runaway mules are friendly creatures except towards their owners. I chat to the owners too, when they come charging up the road. I try to put them in good humour so as to save the mules from a beating; but mule-owners are generally short-tempered and would have me mind my own business.

Most of the people I have mentioned are walkers from necessity. Those who walk for pleasure grow fewer by the day. I don't mean long-distance trekkers or high altitude climbers, who are almost professional in their approach to roads and mountains. I mean people such as myself who are no great athletes but who enjoy sauntering through the woods on a frosty morning, or leaving the main road and slithering downhill into a bed of ferns, or following a mountain stream to reach the small spring in the rocks where it begins.... But no – everyone must have a destination in mind, for this is the age of destinations, be it the Taj Mahal, the casino at Cannes, or the polar ice-cap. I glanced into a bestselling book of records the other day and my eye alighted on an entry which stated that somebody's grandmother had knitted a scarf that was over 20 miles long. Where was it going, I wondered, and who would be wearing it? The book didn't say. It was just another destination, another "first" to be recorded.

Personally I prefer people who come second. I feel safer with them.

It takes a car less than five minutes up the hill to the Bank. It takes me roughly 25 minutes. But there is never a dull moment. Apart from having interesting animal and human encounters, there are the changes that occur almost daily on the hill slopes: the ferns turning from green to gold, the Virginia creepers becoming a dark crimson, horse-chestnuts falling to the ground. And here's a Redstart, come down early from higher altitudes to escape the snows. He whistles cheerfully in a medlar tree. Wild duck flying south – there they go, high over the valley, heading for the lakes and marshlands.

If there's no one on the road, and I feel like a little diversion, I can always sing. I don't sing well, but there's no one to hear me except for a startled woodpecker, so I can go into my Nelson Eddy routine, belting out the songs my childhood gramophone taught me. "Tramp, Tramp, Tramp", "Stouthearted men", "Song of the Open Road"! No one writes marching songs now, so I have to rely on the old ones.

Above me the blue sky, around me the green forest, below me the dusty plains.

Presently I am at *Char Dukan* (Four Shops) and the bank.

I enter the bank, to be greeted effusively by Mr Vishal Ohri, the manager – not because I have come to make a large deposit but because he is that rarity among bank managers, a nature lover! When he learns that I have just seen the first Redstart of the winter, he grows excited and insists that I take him down to it. As it is nearing the tea-break, he sets off with me down the road and, to our mutual satisfaction and delight, the Redstart is still in the medlar tree, putting on a special performance seemingly for our benefit.

The Manager returns to his office, happy to be working at this remote hilltop branch. Both staff and customers will find him the most understanding and sympathetic of managers, for has he not just seen the first white-capped Redstart to fly into Landour, Mussoorie, for the winter? As good a "first" as any in those books of records.

As long as there are nature-loving bank managers, I muse on my way home, there's still hope for this little old world. And for bank depositors too!

Some residents of Landour past and present have been known to be slightly touched. There is a theory that anyone who lives above 7,000 feet starts having delusions, illusions and hallucinations. People who, in the cities, are the models of respectability are known to fling more than stones and insults at each other when they come to live up here. Even those who have grown up and gone away still retain their cattiness. As one whiz kid in the advertising world who had grown up in Mussoorie wrote to one of us: "So, has the earthquake left your walls all cracked up.... Seriously, how were the tremors in good old Muss? Half the buildings, which are collapsing anyway, should have – especially the crumbling ones like Mansaram and all those in the same line! I'm being horrid, but disasters do bring out a perverse glee, don't they... especially when one is only a spectator from a faraway place".

A typical Mussoorie feud can be best exemplified by an elderly bachelor and an ancient spinster living in Barlowgang who should really have married each other years ago. They keep up a verbal feud speaking of each other in derogatory terms. One refers to the other's "pink, green and blue dyed hair", while he refers to her as "a walking newspaper". She insists that he is "death warmed up!" and at times "a stuffed shirt" or a "poached egg on toast". He hears it all, only to say: "The best way to cure her arthritis is with a big hammer!"

At the other end of town, the owner of the Savoy, Nandu Jauhar, gets used to complaints from his customers because of the widely dispersed wings of this historic edifice. Says he: "When a customer orders hot coffee, the bill is always made out for a *cold coffee*".

Meantime, the tradition of murders continues. A double suicide in one hotel; a body tumbling into the room of a honeymooning couple; and another being exhumed from the floor of a third.

Among the many well-known families who are a part of the history of Mussoorie and who still reside here are: Prince Martand Singh of Kapurthala; the Gantzers; the Alwars; the Skinners; the Alters; Ram Chander & Bros.; Lala Mohan Lal & Sons; and the Karanwal family. Most of the shopkeepers of Landour bazaar are descended from the merchants who first came here with the British soldiers and settlers over 180 years ago.

Mussoorie has always remained a poor cousin to Simla, which had its Viceroy. Nainital had its Governor from the United Provinces. Mussoorie remained unofficial – for affairs of the heart. It has always been a gossipy place, as the extracts from the *Miscellany* and the John Lang article will show. Maybe it is too close to the plains and not close enough to the real mountains; but it has never been a dull or boring place.

Landour as it was around the 1900s, there never were that many trees!

Consecrated on 1st May 1840, St. Paul's Church in Landour Cantonment fulfilled the spiritual needs of the red-coats recuperating at Landour's Convalescent Depot. With the generous efforts of an old Woodstock School alumni, it has been immaculately restored.

Birth of a Hill Station

It was due to the conquest of Garhwal by the Gurkhas that indirectly, Mussoorie came into being. About 245 years ago, in 1765 or there-about, the progenitors of the redoubtable Gurkha warriors who now form so distinguished a section of the Indian Army had, under the leadership of Prithi Narain, begun to make themselves felt as a formidable power. They first subdued Kathmandu and Bhatgaon in Nepal proper; and, after Prithi Narain's death, under his widow and brother as regents for his infant son, they extended their conquests westward into Kumaon.

From Kumaon, the Gurkhas carried their invasion into Garhwal. Srinagar, then the capital of Parduman Sah, the Raja of Garhwal, was attacked in February 1803. The Raja retreated and made a futile stand at Barahat (Uttarkashi), but was driven southwards, first into the Dun, and then to Saharanpur. Here he raised a couple of lakhs of rupees by pawning all his property, his throne, and even the sacred jewels and plated the Badrinath temple. With these funds he got together a new army, returned to the Dun, and attacked the invaders who, under Umar Singh Thapa, had occupied Dehra; but he was defeated and killed.

J.B. Fraser, author of *Himalayan Mountains*, mentions that the priests of Paligarh, a sacred glen not far from Jumnotri, prophesied the misfortunes of

Raja Parduman Sah, the rise of Gurkha power and its eventual subjugation by the British. In fact, British forces reached the steep south faces of the Siwalik range just as the Gurkha wave surged up the northern slopes. Colonel Burn marched into Saharanpur about the same time as Umar Singh Thapa occupied Dehra, in October 1803.

The immediate cause of the war between the Gurkhas and the British was the destruction of a police station in a disputed portion of British frontier territory and the barbarous murder of the *daroga* in charge after a gallant defence in which 18 of his constables were killed and six wounded. Another police station was raided shortly afterwards. The season being unfavourable for undertaking punitive operations, the Governor General sent a letter of remonstrance to the Raja of Nepal. The reply was unsatisfactory, even insolent, and war was formally declared on 1 November 1814, although operations had begun before that. The Gurkhas, as might be expected, proved formidable foes, and although they had a mere handful of fighting men in the Dun, they gave the British no end of trouble, and their defence of their hastily constructed fort on the Nalapani hill, better known as Kalinga, was as stubborn and heroic as any such deed that history records. It took three separate assaults by British troops before the Gurkhas were compelled by continuous and well-sustained bombardment to evacuate the Kalinga Fort. In number about 70 survivors only, they cut their way through the besiegers' lines on the night of 30 November.

The gallant Gurkhas afterwards repulsed another British assault under Major Baldock against Jauntgarh, a mountain fort in Jaunsar into which they had thrown themselves. After repulsing this attack Balbhaddar Singh, commander of the Gurkhas, crossed the Jamuna and held Jaitak in Sirmur territory against all British efforts, till the evacuation of all Gurkha strongholds between the Kali and the Sutlej, by treaty, on 15 May 1815. And now the Dun proper, as we know it, may be considered to have come into existence. It was formally annexed to the district of Saharanpur by a Resolution of Government dated 17 November 1815.

Some five years afterwards, in 1822, the Hon. Mr. Shore was appointed Joint Magistrate and Superintendent of the Revenues of the Dun; but some time before that it appears that a force of Military Police, called the Sirmur Battalion, had been raised and equipped from amongst the Sirmurias and the remnants of the Gurkhas left in the Dun, under the command of Captain Young (Captain 'Jung' to the Gurkhas) of the 68th N. I. This battalion was afterwards well-known as the Sirmur Rifles, or the 2nd Prince of Wales' Own Gurkhas, whose headquarters continue to be the cantonments west of Dehra Dun.

It is natural to suppose that officers locate the hills and eventually climb them here and there in search of sport and recreation. The first house erected on the hills north of Dehra was a small hut built on the Camel's Back as a shooting-box by Mr. Shore and Captain Young in 1823. Another small house was built shortly afterwards, somewhere on the Kulri hill. This is said to be Zephyr Cottage, close to Zephyr Hall, now in ruins. Mullingar, built by Captain Young as his residence as Commandant of Landour, and White Park Forest, later known as Annfield (burnt down during riots in 1947), are probably the first houses built which are recognizable in the present day. White, Park and Forest were the names of three men who chummed at the house. The splendid climate and the good sport obtainable gradually attracted other Europeans as the Dun and the hills to the north became better known; in 1827, the government established a convalescent depot for European soldiers at Landour.

By this time there were several houses in Mussoorie: the Park was built by Colonel Wyshe in 1827; Phoenix Lodge in 1829; and about this time Captain Kirke, and one or two others whose names are amongst the first in the old householder's register, commenced building. As it is recorded that a merchant named Lawrence came up in 1829 with a stock of miscellaneous goods for sale, building a hut for himself and his wares on the Camel's Back, there must have been something of a European consumer population by that time.

The two stations of Landour and Mussoorie were at first entirely separate. The convalescent depot was on top of the Landour hill; Mussoorie showed a tendency to keep well to the west in the direction of Hathipaon and Cloud End. The Old Brewery, Bohle's Brewery, and the first school (Mackinnon's) were out west; Colonel Everest, the first Surveyor General who located himself in Mussoorie, fixed on the Park as his office and residence. Clover Lodge, Leopard Lodge, Cloud End, and the ruins of other old houses in that direction show the western tendency of Mussoorie, which was further emphasised by the reservation of sites for bazaars at Hathipaon, at Dudhili Khal and even

Stiffles restaurant was indeed a popular place as seen by the rows of rickshaws lining the Mall Road in those days of ease and leisure. Later it reincarnated as the Standard Skating Rink which was consumed in a fire in the late 1960s.

as far west as Bhadraj, a hill crowned by a temple, overlooking the Jamuna river. Mussoorie and Landour having since joined, and eastern Mussoorie being overbuilt and overcrowded, the western tendency is reasserting itself.

There was apparently no settlement of any kind in Mussoorie or Landour till some 18 years after Captain Young and Mr. Shore built the first hut on the Camel's Back. Indeed, beyond Mr. Calvert's fixing of the Revenue Sub-divisons in 1816, there appeared to have been no regular settlements and surveys in the Dun itself. The European settlers in Mussoorie took up what land they required direct from the *zamindars* of the villages on both slopes of the hills. The boundary line between Dehra Dun and territories with Raja Sudarshan Sah of Tehri, who was reinstated after the British had driven the Gurkhas out of the Dun, was led down as the watershed of the Mussoorie-Landour range. Hence the northern slopes of the hill down towards the Aglar valley were, strictly speaking, Tehri territory. The question of the boundary first cropped up when the government established a convalescent depot at Landour in 1827. Since the land on the northern slopes of the hill was not in British territory, compensation was accordingly determined on by way of annual rent, the government paying Rs. 70 per annum for the Landour depot and for the Civil Station, or Mussoorie proper, Rs. 278 per annum. These rates were later enhanced; but as the total area of Mussoorie and Landour was nearly 20 square miles (about half of which, roughly speaking, was Tehri territory), a rent of roughly Rs. 350 per annum was by no means excessive, about Rs. 35 per square mile!

The first business started in Mussoorie (if we exclude Mr. Lawrence's venture of general goods for sale in 1829) would appear to have been the Old Brewery which was started by Mr. Bohle from Meerut in 1830, on the site of the later Mackinnon's Brewery. In 1832 Mr. Bohle appears to have got into trouble with Colonel Young (Captain Young of Sirmur Rifles), who at this time apparently combined the offices of Superintendent of the Dun and Commandant of Landour. The difficulty seems to have been about supplying beer to soldiers who came down from Landour to the brewery with forged passes. Whether on account of the trouble with the authorities, or because he found that a hill brewery was not a paying concern, Mr. Bohle closed his brewery. Two years later, in 1834, Mr. Mackinnon came up, purchased the estate and opened the first of Mussoorie's schools, calling it the Mussoorie Seminary. Bohle also returned about the same time and reopened the Old Brewery where he continued working till 1838 when he built the place known as Bohle's Brewery. The ruins of this place are still in evidence. Bohle's Bullock Cart Train (from Rajpur to Mussoorie) was famous in its time as a goods carrier. Mr. Bohle's tomb is one of the more impressive monuments in the Camel's Back Cemetery.

In 1835 the European population was large enough to trouble itself about its spiritual needs. A meeting was got up to arrange the erecting of a church and Mr. Mackinnon, already one of the leading men in Mussoorie owing to his energy and public spirit, proposed and selected the site; in 1836, the tower and nave of .the present Christ Church were erected by Captain Rennie Tailour of the Bengal Engineers. The Mussoorie Library also owes its origins (1841) to Mr. Mackinnon; his portrait still hangs in its reference room.

St. Paul's Church was built a short time after the Mussoorie Church and consecrated by Bishop Wilson on 1 May 1840.

Mussoorie's first bank, the North-West Bank, was started in 1836 under the management of Colonel F. Angelo, and for some time it was utilized as a Government bank, holding a floating deposit of treasury money for the convenience of government officers and their families residing in Mussoorie. This arrangement was terminated in 1842 by Mr. Vansittart, then Superintendent of the Dun; it is probable that he was well advised in so doing, as the bank stopped payment shortly afterwards. The depositors were all paid up, but the shareholders lost a good deal. In 1864 the Mussoorie Savings Bank was started by Mr. Hobson, and sometime later the Himalaya Bank was opened under the management of Mr. Moss. These two banks disappeared too, the collapse of the latter creating rather a sensation at the time. Some say Mossy Falls was named after Mr. Moss! The Alliance Bank of Simla opened a branch in Mussoorie on 21 August 1891 in very .handsome premises known as Tiverton House, at the east end of the Mall. This too crashed. Mussoorie was not a healthy place for banks in the good old days!

In 1841 the settlement of Mussoorie was carried out by Mr. Wells, who demarcated and mapped out the various estates taken up by the European settlers. In 1842, after Mr. Wells' settlement, the Mussoorie Municipal Board was constituted and the records of the settlements deposited in their office. The first Secretary was Mr. MacGregor, and the office was initially a room in the *kachehri*, while the monthly meetings were held in the Library, in the Mussoorie Bank, and in various other places. It was not until 1871 that the Belleville estate was purchased by the Municipality and the existing house altered and enlarged to suit the purposes of a Municipal and Town Hall.

Mussoorie seems from the first to have been an eligible residence for Indian princes. The Chateau Kapurthala, the picturesque hill residence of the Maharaja of Kapurthala above the Savoy Hotel is well-known. Mussoorie was also the home of an ex-Amir of Afghanistan, who, with his family and retinue of Kabulis, resided at Bellevue on the southern spur of Vincent's Hill. As far back as 1853 Mussoorie offered shelter for a time to a distinguished Punjabi prince, Maharaja Dalip Singh, son of the celebrated Lion of the Punjab, Ranjit Singh. When the child prince was removed from the Punjab, he was first made over to the care of Dr. Login at Lucknow. Afterwards he was sent up to Mussoorie as he was not keeping good health in the plains, and the Castle, the house on top of Castle Hill, was selected as Dalip Singh's residence.

In 1842 a weekly newspaper called *The Hills* was started by Mr. Mackinnon, who was still very much the moving spirit of Mussoorie. Well-edited and well-supported, it soon made its mark and became well-known. It was decidedly radical in its views and appeared to have adopted the idea of the traditional Irishman, who was not quite sure what his politics were except that they were "agin the Guv'ment anyhow!" However, the Government was able to survive it. The paper ran for some seven or eight years, when Mr. Mackinnon closed his school and reopened his Brewery in 1849. For some years Mussoorie was without a paper of any sort until, in 1860, Dr. Smith revived *The Hills* in a larger form, and it continued till 1865, when it finally collapsed.

About 1870 an attempt was made to start another paper called *The Mussoorie Exchange*. It was chiefly an advertiser and only lived for a few months. In 1872 Mr. Coleman started the *Mussoorie Season* and was joined in this venture by Mr. John Northam, who, when Mr. Coleman disappeared from Mussoorie somewhat abruptly in 1874, ran the paper till the end of the season, and then started *The Himalaya Chronicle*. In the winter of 1875-76 an attempt was made to run *The Himalaya Chronicle* throughout the year, transferring the publication to Meerut during the cold weather, but apparently this was not successful, as it was only tried for one year. After the demise of *The Himalaya Chronicle* there have been several other weekly papers published in Mussoorie from time to time, one of which, *The Beacon*, under Dr. Hawthorne, had a somewhat lurid, but brief career. A pity there are no file copies of most of these old papers, for they would provide a fascinating picture of the Mussoorie of their day.

The indefatigable Mr. Mackinnon also opened the Seminary, Mussoorie's first school, and the hill station rapidly developed on scholastic lines through the 19th and 20th centuries. Several minor schools were started from time to time, flourished for a while and faded away. But the real "boom" in English education took place in independent India. Today, private schools flourish as they never did before.

The Mussoorie Cart Road, generally known as Mackinnon's Road, was commenced in 1843, a joint stock company with a capital of Rs 60,000 being floated by Mr. Mackinnon for the purpose. The road was wonderfully well graded and constructed; passing above Bhatta village, it came up by the Crown Brewery to the Library, a branch going eastward from Kincraig towards Tara Hall. The present motor road simply follows it.

Mussoorie has from its beginning had a curious attraction for surveyors. Colonel Everest, then Surveyor General of India, made his headquarters in the Park as far back as 1832, while the head office of the Great Trignometrical Survey, and the recess quarters of all sorts of survey parties, scientific, topographical and revenue, have constantly been located in Mussoorie. Many a survey officer who subsequently distinguished himself in geodetic work made his first acquaintance with a big 36-inch theodolite in the little observatory on the top of Camel's Back under the paternal guidance of Mr. J.B. Hennessy, for many years in charge of the Head Quarters Office, and afterwards Superintendent of the G.T. Branch of the Department. After the amalgamation of the three separate Survey Departments, Trignometrical, Topographical and Revenue into one, the Headquarters of the Trignometrical Branch were retained in their winter quarters at Dehra Dun.

Mussoorie was first connected by telegraph with the world in general about 1865. A post office had been established with the opening of the Landour Convalescent Depot in 1827. The Head Post Office was for many years at Grand Parade, at the entrance to the Landour bazaar, but with the growing importance of Mussoorie, the opening of a branch office (now the Main Post Office) on the Kulri Hill in the centre of the shopping and business quarters was a real boon to the public.

British presence in India. Railways, roads, bridges, canals and other monuments of engineering and architecture still exist, but the lonely graves with their touching epitaphs of forgotten men and women have a very human story to tell.

The average life-span for a Briton in India during the period 1801-50 was calculated at 31 years for a man and 28 for a woman. Dehra Dun is healthier than most places, but even here one finds the common grave often members of the well-known Powell family from nearby Saharanpur. Within three days they had all died of cholera. Dehra's oldest monument is in the shape of a toy Noah's ark on a plinth. It hears the inscription, "Sacred to the memory of John Graves, son of John Graves, Sgt. Major, Sirmoor Battalion, who died on 9th April, 1820, aged 25 days."

There were, of course, exceptions, among them my great grandmother, Lillian Clerke, who outlived her son and died in Dehra at the age of 86. And across the hills, in the township of Nahan, capital of the former state of Sirmur, is the grave of a lone Englishwoman, Louisa Pearsall, who died in 1921 at the age of 87. The only Europeans in Sirmur were the Raja's medical officers. Although Dr. Pearsall died in 1885, his widow stayed on in this lonely backwater for 38 years in order that she might he buried beside her husband.

Perhaps the most impressive monument in the Dehra cemetery is the one over the grave of Colonel Charles Roberts, Commandant of the 17th Regiment, Irregular Cavalry, Bengal Army, who died at Dehra Dun on 6 July 1873, in his 52nd year. It was erected by an Indian, A.Vyas, "In affectionate memory of his departed friend and benefactor", and consists of a five-foot-high marble angel on a pedestal, with four sandstone pillars on a cut-stone base. The pillars support a sandstone dome which is surmounted by a heavy marble urn.

The inscription on the tomb of Winifred Catherine McMullen reads:

Weep not for me, my husband dear,
But pray and think of me;
As I am now so you must be,
Prepare yourself to follow me.

Thus prevailed upon, the obedient Mr. McMullen joined his wife within a couple of years.

The cemeteries themselves are not haunted places, why should they be? After all, we are already dead (or ought to be) when we are placed in our graves, and our ghosts, if restless, are more likely to visit the places where they lived and breathed and had their being; an old home, a familiar bench. Or, if one has left the world in unhappy circumstances, one might want to revisit the scene of the tragedy to see, perhaps, if things cannot yet be set right....

India is full of British ghosts – the ghosts of soldiers, adventurers, engineers, magistrates, memsahibs, their children, even their dogs! But why so many British ghosts and so few Indian ghosts?

One reason could be that the British, in life, were restless here, so far from the shores of their small green island. And being restless in life, it was only natural that they should remain restless in death.

And then, a burial is not perhaps as final as a cremation. A Christian, interred complete in his parts, may well be tempted to resume his earthly form again!

This does not imply that Hindus do not believe in ghosts. On the contrary, Hindu folklore is overpopulated with spirits of all kinds – *prets* and *bhuts*, all kinds of mischievous ghosts, some living in trees, some in stones, some at the bottom of a well but seldom, if ever, assuming a familiar human form. Very specialised ghosts, these, like the ghost in the peepul tree who waits for the unwary traveller to open his mouth and then jumps down his throat and ruins the poor man's digestion. (Never yawn under a peepul tree!) The one that comes closest to looking human is the *churel* – the ghost of an immoral woman – her only deviation from the norm being that her feet always face backwards.

The Indian hill stations were so very English – and to some extent still are – that it is only natural that they have peopled by English ghosts.

Some of the old houses are in ruins but many still stand and it is understandable if their former owners wish to visit them from time to time. I live in one of these turn-of-the-century buildings on the outskirts of Mussoorie; an old, rather shaky cottage near a forest of oak and rhododendron. There are two floors and for many years the lower rooms were occupied by Miss Ripley-Bean who had spent all her life in the hill station. She had outlived all her relatives. When I came to stay in the upstairs rooms, she was living downstairs with her dog and an old bearer who had been with her for the better part of his life.

Many were the stories she told me of Mussoorie's early days, and a number of her tales were of hauntings, some of them her own experiences – such as the occasion when she was taking a walk on the Camel's Back Road and a gentleman in a top hat and frock coat walked, not past her, but straight through her. She was also accustomed to receive an occasional visit from the ghost of her long dead father, who always wanted to know why she had sold the beautiful house he had built and come to live in this small cottage. Tearfully she would explain that this had been necessary to enable her to look after her invalid sister and retarded brother during their last years, but he never seemed satisfied with this explanation and always went off in a huff.

If anyone is likely to haunt the Mall, it ought to be Mr. James Reginald Clapp, who was murdered on 31 August 1909. The inscription on his tombstone reads: "Murdered by the hand that he befriended". Miss Bean remembered the case quite clearly. She must have been about 27 at the time, and she had met both the victim and his murderer.

Mr. Clapp was an assistant in a chemists' shop of Messrs. J.B. & E. Samuel (it no longer exists under the name), situated in one of the busier parts of the Mall. At that time the adjoining cantonment of Landour was an important convalescent centre for British soldiers. Mr. Clapp was popular with the soldiers and had befriended some of them when they had run short of money. He was a steady worker and sent most of his savings home to his mother in Birmingham; she was planning to use the money to buy the house in which she lived.

The murder was a brutal one, the initial attack being launched with a soda-water bottle on the victim's head. Mr. Clapp's throat was then cut from ear to ear with his own razor. The body was discovered on the floor of the shop the next morning by the proprietor Mr. Samuel, who did not live on the premises.

Suspicion immediately fell on Corporal Alien, who had been particularly friendly with Mr. Clapp. That same night Alien had left Mussoorie for Rajpur in the foothills (a seven mile walk by the bridle-path), arriving at a boarding house several hours later than he was expected. According to some, Mr. Clapp had last been seen in the Corporal's company.

There was other circumstantial evidence pointing to Alien's guilt. On the day of the murder Clapp had received his salary, and this sum, in sovereigns and notes, was never traced. Alien was alleged to have made a payment in sovereigns at Rajpur.

Someone had given Alien a biscuit-tin packed with sandwiches for his journey and it was thought that perhaps the tin had been used by the murderer as a safe for the stolen money. But no tin was ever found and Alien denied having had one with him.

He was arrested at Rajpur and brought back to Mussoorie under escort. There he was taken immediately to the where the body still lay, the police hoping that he might confess his guilt when confronted with the disfigured body of the victim; but Alien was unmoved, except to protest his innocence.

Meanwhile, other soldiers from among Mr. Clapp's friends had collected on the Mall. They were ready to lynch Alien as soon as he was brought out of the shop. The situation was tense, but trouble was averted by the resourcefulness of Mr. Rust, the local photographer, who being of the same build as the Corporal, put on an army coat with a turned-up collar and arranged to be handcuffed between two policemen. He remained with them inside the shop, in partial view of the mob of soldiers, while the rest of the police party escorted the Corporal out by the back door. Mr. Rust did not abandon his disguise or leave the shop until word arrived that Alien was secure in the police station.

Corporal Alien was found guilty and hanged at Naini Jail, far from Mussoorie. But there were many who felt that his guilt had never really been proved and that he had been convicted on purely circumstantial evidence. Looking back at the case from this distance in time, one cannot help feeling that the soldier might have been a victim of circumstances, and perhaps of local prejudice, for he was not liked by his fellows.

Allen himself hinted that he was not in the vicinity of the crime that night but in the company of a lady whose good name he was determined to shield. (Perhaps it was she who had given him the sandwiches packed in the biscuit-tin.) If this was true, it was a pity that the lady prized her virtue more than her friend's life, for she did not come forward to save him. In 1909, of course, virtue counted for a great deal more than it does today. Miss Bean shared the general dislike of the Corporal and believed he was guilty but admitted that the case against him was not a strong one. The Chaplain who administered to Corporal Alien during his last days in the condemned cell was prepared to absolve him of the crime. He never accepted that Alien was a murderer.

So, perhaps it is the Corporal's ghost, rather than Mr. Clapp's which haunts the Mall. The Mall is full of ghosts. They are there on misty monsoon nights, when the lamplight struggles to penetrate the gloom. Mr. Rust's ghost may well be about, too, for he died here in the 1920s, "mourned by all who knew him", including Miss Bean who had been photographed by him, several times.

Miss Bean had been quite beautiful in her youth (I have an early photograph taken in 1895), and even in her old age she had a smooth soft skin, a straight back, generous hips and shapely feet. She had taken rather a fancy to me, partly because I shared my tins of sardines with her, and partly because I reminded her of some lost childhood friend.

She died in her 90th year. Although she had given her own people sumptuous funerals, there was no one to give her one, and she was buried with the help of the Church Benevolent Society. For years she had been living on the income from a small investment of her father, supplemented by food parcels from an old friend who had settled in New Zealand. At the time of her death I was having my own struggles and could do nothing about the funeral except attend it. But I'm glad I had been able to share my sardines with her.

Miss Bean is still very much a part of this cottage. I do not see her ghost. Nor do I hear strange sounds or comings and goings. But sometimes in the early hours, when sleep is fitful and uneasy and a restless wind wanders around the cottage, I am dimly aware of someone tucking me up in bed, smoothing down the pillow, rearranging the counterpane....

I turn over peacefully, knowing that it is only Miss Bean trying to ensure that I get a good night's sleep.

The romance of the rickshaws.

Victorian party games consisted of word games, all complete with booklet and attached pencil.

Tales of a Hill Station

Visitors to Mussoorie frequently find themselves persuaded to take the ropeway to the top of a local peak called Gun Hill from where they are able to enjoy a view of both the plains and the Greater Himalayas. They will also see the Mussoorie waterworks; but of a gun there is no sign, and they may be pardoned for wondering how the hill acquired its impressive name.

Before 1919, the Mussoorie public used to be told the time at noon by the firing of a gun from the peak known as Gun Hill. Perhaps guns were cheaper than clocks in those days; I cannot think of any other sound reason for the system. It was not very popular with the local residents. At first the gun faced east, but soon after its installation (shortly after 1857), Miss Bryan of Grey Castle Nursing Home and then Miss Hamilton of the same institution complained that when the gun was fired "it often loosed plaster from the ceiling of the wards, which fell on the patients' beds and unnerved them". It could not be pointed north, because it would then have blasted away Mr. Yerborough's house, Dilkusha; so it was faced north-east, and almost immediately came a complaint from Crystal Bank. Turned to the south, it almost succeeded in fulfilling its legitimate duty: the gunner forgot to remove the ramrod from the barrel; and on booming noon to the populace, the cannon sent the ramrod clean through the roof of Stella Cottage.

The Happy Valley Club was set up in 1904 by V.A. Mackinnon with a race course, library and tennis courts -- indeed a most happening place till it wound up in 1947.

Public opinion was now mounting against the gun, and it was turned around once more, to face the Mall. Its boom was usually produced by ramming a mixture of moist grass and cotton waste down the barrel, after the powder was in place. Due to an accidental overcharge of powder, one of these canon-balls landed with some force on the lap of a lady who was being taken by a dandy down to the plains. It was the last straw – or to be exact, the last straw canon- ball – for the gun was dismantled soon after this incident.

A peep into the life of a hill station before the turn of the century provides us with much interesting matter on European social life during that period. But before giving the reader further anecdotes, I should fill in the background with a brief historical sketch of Mussoorie.

In the year 1825, the Superintendent of the Doon was a certain Mr. F.J. Shore who found time from his official duties to scramble up to the hills then known as *Mansuri* because of the prevalence of a shrub known in the vernacular as the Mansur plant. He found that these hills had a number of flat areas, some of which accommodated the huts of cowherds who grazed their cattle on them during the summer months. Game was then plentiful in the hills, and the first construction was a shooting-box built jointly by Mr. Shore and Captain Young of the Sirmur Rifles. The first home, still recognizable was Mullingar on Landour Hill, built in 1826 by Captain Young. Soon Landour became a convalescent depot for British troops, and settlers began flocking to Mussoorie, building houses as far apart as Cloud End in the west, and Dahlia Bank in the east, separated by a distance of some 12 miles. In 1832 Colonel Everest (after whom the mountain is named) as Surveyor General opened his Survey of India office in The Park and made a road to it. Mussoorie is the original home of the department.

People came to Mussoorie for both business and pleasure, and amongst the pleasure seekers we find the Hon'ble Emily Eden, sister of Lord George Eden, Earl of Auckland, Governor General of India. In her journals she records that "in the afternoon we took a beautiful ride up to Landour, but the paths are much narrower on that side, and our courage somehow oozed out, and first we came to a place where they said 'this was where poor Major Blundell and his pony fell over, and they were both dashed to atoms' – and then there was a board stuck in a tree 'From this spot a Private in the Cameroons fell and was killed'.... We had to get off our ponies and lead them and altogether I thought much of poor Major Blundell! But it is impossible to imagine more beautiful scenery." Though there were no proper roads in Mussoorie in those pioneer days, it is probably safe to assume that a number of cliff-edge accidents were caused by the beer that was then so cheap and plentiful in the hill station.

However, the big push in the brewery business really began in 1876, when everyone suddenly acclaimed a much improved brew. The source was traced to Vat 42 in Whymper and Company's Crown Brewery. The beer was re-tasted and re-tasted until the diminishing level of the barrel revealed the perfectly brewed remains of a human being! Someone, probably drunk, had fallen into the beer barrel and been drowned and, all unknown to himself, had given the beer trade a real fillip. Apocryphal though this story may sound, I have it on the authority of *A Mussoorie Miscellany*. Its author goes on to say that "meat was thereafter recognised as the missing component and as scrupulously added till more modern and less cannibalistic means were discovered to satiate the froth-blower."

A bold, bad place was Mussoorie in those days, according to the correspondent of *The Statesman*, who in his paper of 22 October 1884, wrote "Ladies and gentlemen, after attending church, proceed to a drinking shop, a restaurant adjoining the Library, and there indulge freely in pegs, not one but many; and at a Fancy Bazaar held this season, a lady stood up on her chair and offered her kisses to gentlemen at Rs. 5 each. What would they think of such a state of society at home?"

Fortunately, a *Statesman* correspondent was not present at a 1932 benefit show, when a Mussoorie lady stood up and auctioned a single kiss, for which a gentleman paid Rs. 300!

The famous traveller Lowell Thomas, visiting Mussoorie in 1926, wrote: "There is a hotel in Mussoorie (The Savoy) where they ring a bell just before dawn so that the pious may say their prayers and the impious, get back to their own beds."

When a famous clairvoyant and crystal-gazer, Lady Ormes by Gore, was murdered in her suite at the Savoy (her crystal-ball having let her down for once), Rudyard Kipling sent details of the crime to his friend Arthur Conan Doyle. But even the creator of Sherlock Holmes could not solve this particular mystery. The poisoner was never discovered and her doctor was later found dead in mysterious circumstances.

As early as 1827, Capt. Young instinctively knew the importance of the mail to the troops recuperating at the Convalescent Depot and started the Landhaur Post Office in today's Chowk.

A view of the main promenade of the Mall shows the very heart of its commercial centre in the Kulri.

In spite of these goings-on, or perhaps because of them, the inhabitants were conscious of their spiritual needs and a number of churches were soon dotted about the hill station. The oldest of these is Christ Church (1836) whose chaplain almost a hundred years later was the fair-minded Reverend T.W. Chisolm. In his usual Sunday service prayers in the year 1933, he sought God's help for Pandit Motilal Nehru who was then seriously ill. There was an immediate storm in all official teacups and the chaplain was reprimanded. This caused one local writer of the time to comment "that in these years of our Lord, Holy Orders can be interpreted to mean wholly Government orders."

Another public-spirited Mussoorie citizen was Captain A.W. Hearsey (a member of the famous Hearsey family which had once owned large areas of the Dun). He was one of the first Anglo-Indian members of the Indian Congress. He had spoken at an All-India Congress Session, and a certain English language newspaper, in its report of the proceedings, referred to him as "a brown man who called himself a military captain". Without any delay, Captain Hearsey armed himself with a horse-whip, made a long train

The present State Bank of India building is housed in the erstwhile Himalaya Hotel.

journey, and descended on the offices of the newspaper. On finding that the reporter in question was away on furlough he said the editor would suit his purpose equally, and bursting into the editor's office proceeded to horsewhip him. The litigation that followed evoked widespread interest at the time.

When Jawaharlal Nehru came to Mussoorie in 1920, he had not yet entered politics; but as a result of an incident in Mussoorie he was soon to find himself in the thick of the freedom struggle.

In May 1920, Pandit Jawaharlal Nehru's mother and wife were not keeping well and he brought them (and his infant daughter Indira) up to the salubrious climate of Mussoorie. They stayed at the Savoy. Also staying there was a delegation from Afghanistan which was in India for political talks with the British government. Pandit Nehru did not know about the Afghans until after his arrival; but the government, fearing that he might try to contact them and influence them in some way, asked him to sign an undertaking that he would not get in touch with any of the delegates. This he refused to do. He was not really interested in meeting the Afghans but he insisted that no one had the right to prevent him from doing so.

Ordered by the authorities to leave Mussoorie within 24 hours, he kept his wife and mother at the Savoy with instructions for them to continue their medical treatment, and returned to Allahabad. Having no other engagements just then, he decided to visit a few hundred farmers who were camping on the banks of the Yamuna under the leadership of Baba Ramchandra. They appealed to him to help free them from the coils of greedy landlords who were overtaxing them and making it difficult for them to earn a living. It was his first real contact with the masses. For the first time he realised where his true sympathies lay – with the poor of India – and from then on his life was to take a new direction.

After India's independence in 1947, Mussoorie went through a difficult period. The British had gone and the wealthy princes and landowners were also finding times difficult. Hotels and boarding houses began to close down. Then, in the early sixties the prosperous Indian middle classes became hill station conscious and once again crowds thronged the Mall on summer evenings. Now, in the twenty-first century, the foreign tourist is discovering the delights of the lower Himalayas.

It is easy enough to get to Mussoorie today, but how did they manage it before the advent of the railway and the automobile? Of course Mr. Shore and Captain Young merely scrambled up the goat tracks to get there; and Lady Eden used her pony to canter along paths and "up precipices", but in the good old, old days (before the turn of the century), one detrained at Ghaziabad (some 150 miles from one's destination), engaged a village bullock cart, and proceeded in the direction of the Siwaliks as fast as only a bullock cart can go. After that, one walked, rode a pony, or was carried uphill in a doolie.

Later, the bullock cart gave way to the *dak ghari,* and the tonga and soon after the opening of the Hardwar-Dehra railway in 1901, the tonga was ousted by the motor car and bus. Up to that time, the main overnight stop was at Rajpur, not Dehra, and the hostelries and forwarding agencies at Rajpur were the Ellenborough Hotel, the Prince of Wales Hotel and the Agency Retiring Rooms of Messrs Buckle and Company's Bullock Train Agency. They are all now in ruins.

The only edifices in the vicinity of this hill station that might pass muster as "ancient monuments" are the impressive ruins of the old breweries. They have fallen down – sad reminders of the gay days when beer was less than a rupee a bottle, and only kisses were expensive.

The Schools Today

Mussoorie's first school we know to have been Mr. MacKinnon's Seminary. When the founder closed the institution and re-opened the Old Brewery, Mr. Ramsay took over the school, but for some reason it was not a success. Then Reverend Maddock, at that time Chaplain of Mussoorie, sent for his brother from England and he started a school on the hill above the Liberty, where the Savoy Hotel now is. The institution was known as Maddock's School.

The next local school to open was the Convent of Jesus and Mary, Waverley which was started in 1845. It had its formal opening on 18 September, not in March as we have it now. Waverley was the second school to be established in India by the religious of the Congregation of Jesus and Mary. It was the first of the Convent boarding schools in the Northern provinces.

Waverley became a first class boarding school, chiefly for the daughters of officers. Belmont was run as a second class boarding school for a short while and then became a junior School. Thistle Bank was, and still is, the Chaplain's residence.

The first community consisted of five nuns of whom Mother Gonzaga was the Superior, and they arrived from Dehradun in bullock carts - a very different mode of transport from our comfortable school van! Through the years it was necessary to make changes and additions to the buildings as the original ones

The Mussoorie School was started at the present site of the Savoy Hotel by Reverend Maddock in 1865.

were almost completely destroyed in the great earthquake of 1905. Further additions and improvements were made by the different Superiors as the years went by.

In the month of January 1853 Mgr. Carli bought the property of Manor House from Mr. Hutton and in the same year the first Principal Rev. Fr. Barry received students and began classes. The school was called St. George's School. St. Fidelis' School began in 1863 when 29 children were transferred from the Catholic Orphan Asylum at Simla. Fr. Macken was Principal of both schools until the year 1868. Many of the dormitories and classrooms were built during his time.

In the year 1873 Fr. James Doogan came to Manor House. He remained Principal of both schools until the year 1893. He was a very capable and popular man. He improved the buildings, increased the number of students and raised the standard of education.

In 1893, due to increasing missionary work and shortage of priests, both schools were handed over to the Patrician Brothers, and the institution dedicated to the education of youth. The first brother to become Principal was Bro. Stapleton. He was Principal of both schools for one year. In 1894 Bro. Stapleton was succeeded in St. Fidelis' by Bro. Burn but remained Principal of St. George's. Bro. Haverty succeeded Bro. Stapleton at St. George's and remained the principal for many years. He levelled the top of the hill and made what is now the largest flat in Mussoorie.

The facade which gives St. George's such a majestic appearance from every corner of Mussoorie was built by Bro. Phelan. He was a good architect and enriched the school with additional buildings; many of the huge *pustas* protecting the building and roads were built by him.

In 1948 the two schools were amalgamated and called St. George's College. The Patrician Brothers completed a century at Barlowganj in 1993.

The history of Woodstock school begins in 1854. In that year, four ladies from the "London Society for Promoting Female Education in the East" landed in Calcutta and began the long journey up to Mussoorie. They had come in response to an appeal from a committee in Mussoorie consisting of three army officers, the Chaplain of Mussoorie and two American missionaries. Their aim was to start a Protestant Christian School of a quality equivalent to that of Waverley Convent, which had opened in 1854.

The school opened in Cainville Estate. One year later, in 1855, it moved to the other end of Mussoorie, to the Woodstock Estate, where it has continued without a break ever since. The house named Woodstock had been constructed in 1842 by Col. Reilly. In 1867 after Col. Reilly's death, the school purchased the estate from his widow.

The estate adjacent to Woodstock, known as Midlands, was owned by Mr. George Taylor of the East India Company, after whom Taylor's flat is named. In the first decade of the 20th century, Woodstock School was expanding and a teacher's training college was added to the school. To accommodate the college, Woodstock purchased the Midlands Estate and expanded the old to house the college. The college building closed in 1935 and the building became the senior girls' hostel, Midlands, a function which continues to this day.

Woodstock School in 2009 had a strength of 645 pupils – all boarders – from 30 different nationalities and an international set of teachers. The school is still predominantly American in character; its alumni are to be found holding responsible posts in the U.S.A., India and many other countries. All those who have studied at Woodstock have fond memories of the Woodstock grounds which extend down to the streams on each side of Midlands, and which contain a wonderful variety of trees, including oak, chestnut and rhododendron.

The conflict referred to above is evident when we are told that in 1865 Maddock's School, that is the original Mussoorie School, was purchased by the Diocesan Board and placed under the charge of Reverend A.O. Hardy, who was succeeded by the Reverend Stokes, from when the school was known, and is still spoken of, as Stokes School. The school eventually closed in 1901-02 and the popular Savoy Hotel was opened on the site.

At the same period, 1876-77 Hampton Court School was started as a strictly undenominational institution and was conducted by the Rev. Henry Sells. In 1895, it was bought over by Miss Holland and after that it was known as Miss

Balahissar – today's Wynberg Allen School – was home to the exiled Afghan kings. (Picture c.1880.)

Holland's School. Miss Holland, the first Latin M. A. of the Bengal University, won the Roychand Premchand Grant and coming to Mussoorie, started a school at Arundel but bought Hampton Court the next year. Hampton Court was once the Calcutta Hotel and the illiterate therefore called the school the "Calcuttiya School". In 1922 the nuns of Jesus and Mary took it over, and it has since been a boarding school for boys under 12 years of age, and a day school for boys and girls. The Mother Superior at present is the Reverend Mother Mary Xavier.

One of the oldest schools in Mussoorie, Wynberg-Allen was founded more than 100 years ago when a few Christian friends, led by Mr & Mrs Arthur Foy, Brigadier Corden and Mr Alfred Powell, got together in Kanpur to discuss how best to meet the needs of the poor and orphan children of the European and Anglo-Indian communities of North India. From this meeting emerged the idea of an orphanage-cum-training school run on Christian non-sectarian principles.

The school started, in 1886, in a very small way with six pupils, in Rockville one of Mussoorie's oldest buildings situated near Jabarkhet on a hill a few kilometres out of Mussoorie town. The first headmistress, Mrs. Barton-West, took no salary and spent the remainder of her life in improving the school and its standards.

From these humble beginnings the institution gradually acquired more students and staff, and with the help of generous donations from interested persons was able to purchase Wynberg Estate, overlooking the Doon Valley and the Siwalik hills, on the main road to Rajpur and Dehra Dun.

The first Railway Hill school to be started in the Mussoorie area was by S. P. & D. Railway in the 1870s by taking over a small bungalow viz. Fairlawn which was close to the land where Oak Grove was later built. With the change in the name of the railway the school became known as North Western Railway School, Fairlawn Mussoorie. This school remained small, short staffed and had inadequate accommodation. The number of boys and girls on its rolls in the infant classes and from standard I to VII remained less than 40. The school, however, showed some progress during the principalship of Mr. John Buchart with Mrs. Buchart acting as its first Headmistress. North Western Railway resisted the pressure for the school being amalgamated with the East Indian Railway's Hill School (Oak Grove); which started in 1888, till the end of 1891. With the sudden death of Mr. Buchart, the Fairlawn School was finally closed and the staff and students were transferred to Oak Grove School.

When the East India Railway decided to start a Hill School, the School Committee selected for this purpose the Oak Grove Estate, which comprises 193 acres of land, a most picturesque spot at an elevation of 5,300 ft., three miles from Rajpur, on the Rajpur-Mussoorie bridal-path. A good supply of water had been obtained by the acquisition of rights to the water issued from five springs, known as Mossy Falls which rise considerably higher up in the hills, compared to Oak Grove and another adjacent spring. Powell Committee thoughtfully considered that an educational institution could not be a paying proposition or even self-supporting and, therefore, while recommending the proposal for setting up a High School to the companies of Board of Directors, the Agent clearly mentioned: "It would not be prudent to spend money on the school buildings on the assumption that the school will be self supporting."

On the recommendation of the school committee, the Hill School endowment fund of Rs. 2 lakhs was set up to meet from its income, the salaries of the school staff.

The first school building at Oak Grove was designed by the late Mr. R. Soskell Bayne, the Company's Chief Architect, and built under the supervision of the late W. Drysdale, one of the Company's engineers. The original building was meant for both boys and girls, boys being placed at one end and girls at the other. On 19 May 1888, Mr. & Mrs. A.C. Chapman joined the school as its first Headmaster and Headmistress.

At present Oak Grove School consists of three separate schools, a junior school for girls and boys from classes III to V and separate senior schools for boys and girls from classes VI to XII. Each school has its own comfortable and airy dormitories, classrooms and dining halls. The Principal of the combined schools now is Mr. H.P. Watts.

In 1888 Mr. T.H. Garlah started a school in Willow Lodge but moved in 1898 to The Dingle, and later, in 1905, moved again to the present site Woodlands, which is why the school is now known by that name. T.H. Garlah is still proprietor and principal of the institution, which makes a speciality of giving an excellent grounding in school life while living in a real home.

Of all Mussoorie's schools Vincent Hill School is the most unconventional. Organised and managed by the Seventh Day Adventist Mission, it was started in Annfield and later moved to its present site on Vincent Hill whence it adopted its present name. Although the curriculum is not dissimilar to that in most

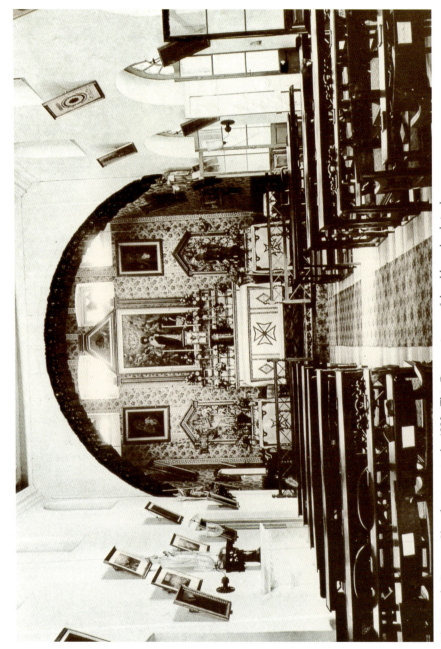

The *Waverly Convent* Chapel as it was in the 1890s. This Convent is one of the oldest schools in the country.

educational institutions, many of the students are trained for Holy Orders, or for colportage. Unlike other schools at Mussoorie Vincent Hill strives to rely as little as possible on hired labour, and pupils are therefore given considerable training in manual and household duties. The excellent products from the school bakery, which were hawked around the station, were testimony to what the students were capable of in the culinary department.

Of the Indian Schools the Ghananand High School and the Islamia School are the biggest. The former was begun 1927 at Thespic Lodge behind the Landour Bazaar, where the Islamia School is now situated, and in 1928 moved to Kincraig where, in spite of being far from the majority of Indian residences of the station, it continues to flourish.

The Islamia School was begun in a tiny room near the Juma Masjid in Landour Bazaar, by Maulvi Md. Sayid in 1906, and was managed up to 1915 by a Committee. In 1916 it came under the management of the Anjuman Islamia and was given Government recognition in 1935.

The Arya Kanya Pathshala was started in 1917 by B. Ram Chandra M.W.S., S.D.O., Landour (now M.E.S. Retired) and after shifting several times to different places was moved to the present Arya Samaj Building near the Dingle. With over 800 students, the school is known for its extra-curricular activities and the National Cadets Corps training.

The Sanatan Dharm Kanya Pathshala was started in 1928 by the Sanatan Dharm Sabha in the building adjoining the Sanatan Dharm Mandir in Landour bazaar.

There have been many other schools that have now been almost forgotten. Amongst these were Philander Smith School, long since moved to Nainital where it continues to flourish; the Junior Mussoorie School once in The Abbey; the Modern School of Bassett Hall; Mr. Moore's Landour Boarding and Day School of Sunny Bank; and later Mullingar; and Mr. Sheehan's Academy where the Civil Hospital now stands.

In recent years a number of new schools have prospered – Mussoorie Modern, Mussoorie Public, Mussoorie International, and the Central School for Tibetans. An English medium education continues to be in great demand. But the two Hindi girls' schools – Mussoorie Girls and Sanatan Dharam – have an excellent reputation. The Mussoorie Post-Graduate College, now in its sixth decade, is a boon to students from both Mussoorie and the surrounding villages.

# Up at the Top

A few years ago I spent a couple of summers up at Sisters Bazaar, at the farthest extremity of Mussoorie's Landour Cantonment – an area as yet untouched by the tentacles of a bulging, disoriented octopus of a hill station.

There were a number of residences up at Sisters, most of them old houses separated from each other by clumps of oak or stands of deodar. After sundown, flying-foxes swooped across the roads, and the nightjar set up its nocturnal chant. Here I thought, I would live like Thoreau at Walden Pond – alone, aloof, far from the strife and cacophony of the vast amusement park that was now Mussoorie. How wrong I was proved to be!

To begin with, I found that almost everyone on the hill side was busily engaged in writing a book. Was the atmosphere really so conducive to creative activity, or was it just a conspiracy to put me out of business? The discovery certainly put me out of my stride completely, and it was several weeks before I could write a word.

There was a retired Brigadier who was writing a novel about World War II, and a retired Vice-Admiral who was writing a book about a Rear Admiral. Mrs. S, who had been an actress in the early days of the talkies, was writing poems in the manner of Wordsworth; and an ageing (or rather, resurrected) ex-

The Bridge at Church Flat near Char Dukan just after it was commissioned to create the Upper Mall.

Maharani was penning her memories. There was also an elderly American who wrote salacious best-selling novels about India. It was said of him that he looked like Hemingway and wrote like Charles Bronson.

With all this frenzied literary activity going on around me, it wasn't surprising that I went into shock for some time.

I was saved (or so I thought) by a 'far-out' ex-hippie and ex-Hollywood scriptwriter who decided he would produce a children's film based on one of my stories. It was a pleasant little story, and all would have gone well if our producer friend hadn't returned from some high-altitude poppy fields in a bit of a trance and failed to notice that his leading lady was in the family way. Although the events of the story all took place in a single day, the film itself took about four months to complete, with the result that her figure altered considerably from scene to scene until, by late evening of the same day, she was displaying all the glories of imminent motherhood.

Naturally, the film was never released. I believe our producer friend now runs a health-food restaurant in Sydney.

I shared a large building (it had paper-thin walls), with several other tenants, one of whom, a French girl in her thirties, was leaning to play the sitar. She and her tabla-playing companion would sleep by day, but practice all through the night, making sleep impossible for me or anyone else in my household. I would try singing operatic arias to drown her out, but you can't sing through all night and she always outlasted me. Even a raging forest fire, which forced everyone else to evacuate the building for a night, did not keep her from sitar any more than Rome burning kept Nero from his fiddle. Finally I got one of the chowkidar's children to pour sand into her instrument, and that silenced her for some time.

Another tenant who was there for a short while was a Dutchman, (yes, we were a cosmopolitan lot in the 1980s before visa regulations were tightened) who claimed to be an acupuncturist. He showed me his box of needles and promised to cure me of the headaches that bothered me from time to time. But before he could start the treatment, he took a tumble while coming home from a late night party and fell down the *khud* into a clump of cacti, the sharp-pointed kind, which punctured the more tender parts of his anatomy. He had to spend a couple of weeks in the local mission hospital, receiving more conventional treatment, and he never did return to cure my headaches.

How did Sisters Bazaar come by its name?

Well, in the bad old, good days when Landour was a convalescent station for sick and weary British soldiers, the nursing sisters had their barracks in the long, low building that lines the road opposite Prakash's Store. On the old maps this building is called 'The Sisters'. For a time it belonged to Dev Anand's family, but I believe it had since changed hands.

Of a 'bazaar' there is little evidence, although Prakash's Store must be at least a hundred years old. It is famous for its home-made cheese and tradition has it that several generations of the Nehru family have patronized the store, from Motilal Nehru in the 1920s, to Rahul and his mother in more recent times.

I am more of a jam-fancier myself, and although I no longer live in the area, I do sometimes drop into the store for a can of raspberry or apricot or plum jam, made from the fruit brought here from the surrounding villages.

Further down the road is Dahlia Bank, where dahlias once covered the precipitous slope behind the house known as the 'Eyebrow'. The old military hospital, (which was opened in 1827) has been altered and expanded to house the present Institute of Technology Management. Beyond it lies Mount Hermon, with the lonely grave of a lady who perished here one wild and windy winter, one-hundred and seventy years ago. And close by lies the lovely Oakville Estate, where at least three generations of the multi-talented Alter family have lived. They do everything from acting in Hindi films to climbing greasy poles, Malkhumb-style. From wise old Bob to Steve and Andy, those Alter boys are mighty handy.

It is cold up there in winter, and I now live about 500 feet lower down, where it is only slightly warmer. But my walks take me up the hill from time to time. Most of the unusual eccentric people I have written about have gone away, but others, equally interesting, have taken their place. But I am saving it for my autobiography. The Mussoorie gossips will then get a dose of their own medicine. Let them start having sleepless nights.

# Looking for John Lang

I had lived in Mussoorie, a hill station in northern India, for over four years without realising that someone of literary distinction might be buried in the old English cemetery. Just as I was about to go away, a friend in Australia sent me a newspaper clipping which made mention of the first Australian-born novelist, John Lang, who spent the last years of his life in Mussoorie and was known to have been buried here. There is still an unsolved mystery about Lang's manuscripts. He left his papers to his second wife, nee Margaret Wetter, but neither they, nor any trace of her after his death, have ever been found.

John Lang was born in Sydney in 1816. His father, a young soldier turned merchant, died before his birth. His mother was Elizabeth Harris, born on Norfolk Island, the daughter of two convicts. Lang proved a brilliant Latin scholar at Sydney College, and then went to England to study law. He was expelled from Cambridge for *Botany Bay Tricks* - believed to be the writing of blasphemous litanies - but was admitted to the Society of the Middle Temple and called to the bar in 1841. He returned to Sydney shortly afterwards, but his convict connections stood in the way of his advancement, and it was only when he went to India that he began to lead a successful legal and literary life. *The Forger's Wife* - a robust tale of Australian outlaws - was published in England in 1855. *Botany Bay* – a collection of stories based on life in Sydney in the early years of the century – was written for Charles Dickens' magazine *Household Words* and published in 1859. The best of his books on India are *Ike Weatherbys(1853)* and *The Ex-Wife* (1859). These take a lightly satirical look at English social life in India, and are precursors of Kipling's stories of Simla society.

Lang practiced at the Bar in Calcutta, and represented the Rani of Jhansi in her legal battles against the East India Company. He did well both as a barrister and as a newspaper proprietor. But none of his manuscripts, and no portrait of him, have ever been discovered. When he died he left everything to his second wife, whom he married in Mussoorie in 1861; but what happened to her after his death remains a mystery.

Although Lang's books are elusive, I decided that his grave should not be so hard to find, and set out in search of it on a crisp October morning. This is the best time of year in the hills, with the grass still fresh and green, the horse-chestnut leaves yellowing, and the hillsides sprinkled with wild geranium and umbrella-fronds of lady's lace.

I take the Camel's Back Road that leads round the northern and more forested face of Gun Hill, which is a rare rocky outcrop in the centre of the hill station. Gun Hill is so named because in Lang's time it boasted a cannon which boomed out at noon each day. The gun, as has earlier been recorded, was a mixed blessing. Once on a Sunday morning during service in the small Anglican Church of St. Thomas (built in 1834 and now beginning to crumble), one of Fisher's cannon-balls shot through the open door, bounced off a pew, and landed in the lap of a stout lady who had been sleeping through the sermon. Fisher was finally relieved of his job, and the cannon was shifted to the municipal godowns where, for all I know, it may still be gathering rust.

Although Mussoorie's Camel Back Road was not as high in social hierarchy as Scandal Point in Simla, it was, until the 1930s, almost exclusively an European preserve; and so was the cemetery, where most of the names on the tombstones are of Anglo-Saxon vintage. The graves occupy terraced slopes which face the snow-covered Nilkanth and Bandarpoonch ranges.

I am unable to enter at the gate which is securely padlocked and encircled by barbed-wire, making the two large notice-boards ("No Trespassing" and

"Visitors Should Leave Their Dogs Behind") seem rather unnecessary. I walk along the railings until I notice a small footpath leading off the verge. Climbing over the railings, I start down the path; but it is steep and slippery with pine needles, and I end by tobogganing down the slope into a thicket of myrtle. Brushing dust, burrs and pine-needles from my clothes, I stand up and survey the hillside, my eyes finally coming to rest on a small knoll where several bulky obelisks rise from the ground. Obelisks were all the rage in the late 19th century, and it is just possible that John Lang's grave will be among them.

The knoll does seem to be the oldest part of the cemetery; it is certainly the prettiest. The sunlight, penetrating the gaps in the tall trees, plays chess on the gravestones, shifting slowly and thoughtfully across the worn old stones. The wind, like a hundred violins, plays perpetually in the topmost branches of the deodars. The only living thing in sight is an eagle, wheeling high overhead. The snows are just a great dazzle in the sky. This is a romantic spot, a fit burial ground for adventurers and pioneers. Here are the graves of soldiers, merchants and evangelists.

Unless John Lang left his widow in a generous mood, the chances of my finding his grave are rather remote. Only the more expensive gravestones with marble insets have retained their inscriptions. The sandstone graves are now just anonymous slabs. Over a hundred monsoons have worn away the lettering on many old tombs.

I am still searching the knoll when I am hailed by a man holding a bundle of sticks in one hand and an axe in the other. He calls out to me in a belligerent tone:

"What are you doing here? And how did you get in?"

"I am looking for a grave," I reply mildly.

"You may come across your own grave, if you walk in here without permission!"

This must be the *mali*, who is both gardener and caretaker. I have been warned about him; a fierce man who has been known to eject intruders at the point of a *lathi*. I am told he is short-sighted; and, like a bear, which is also short-sighted, believes that there is no point in trying to identify an intruder until he has been finished off. It is only when the *mali* comes closer, and finds that I look fairly respectable, that his bluster disappears.

"Some people come here to rob the graves," he explains in an injured tone." And every time an arm or a head or a piece of marble goes," he says, gesturing towards a decapitated angel, "the Committee-*memsahibs* take me to task for carelessness."

"Well, I'll tell the *memsahibs* how vigilant you are. I am looking for an old grave. Over a hundred years old."

"There are some old ones near my house," he says, beginning to mellow. "But you should look at the register, sahib. That will help you find your relative's grave."

I am about to tell him that it is not a relative's grave, then decide not to as I do not want to raise his suspicions again. And it is pleasant to invent a relationship with another writer, a fellow Anglo-Indian or Indo-Anglian, who lived, loved, died and was buried here over a hundred years ago.

"Who has the register?"

"The Garlah miss-sahib. She will tell you everything."

"All right, I'll see her and come again tomorrow."

"If you bring a chit from the miss-sahib, I can open the gate for you."

I continue searching on my own for a while, to the evident unease of the *mali*. Does he really think I shall make off with a headstone?

That evening I visit Miss Garlah. She is a tubby little Anglo-Indian lady with a hearty manner and a strong constitution. Forty of her sixty years have been spent in Mussoorie.

"Did you have trouble with the *mali?*" she asks with apparent relish. Evidently she looks forward to getting complaints about him.

"He was a bit aggressive," I say. "He needs glasses to help him separate grave robbers from other people."

"Well, he saw you climbing the railings, and that made him wonder what you were up to."

"So he's been to you already?"

"Yes, he's very good. We keep him because he's so tough. The last man used to let in all sorts of people, including some hippies who thought the cemetery would be just the right place for smoking pot."

When I tell her the object of my search, she says: "Yes, I have a register. Give me the name and date of your author's death and we'll look him up."

"John Lang. 1864."

"Ah, that's going too far back. There must have been a register for those years, but if there was, it's long since lost. I can help you from 1910 onwards."

I make no attempt to hide my disappointment. "Nothing earlier? If only I had an idea of where the grave might be situated, I might be able to identify it."

"Well, young man, I can only suggest that you keep hunting. Try the graves near the *mali's* house. I'll ask him to clean them up for you. You may be lucky. We do our best to maintain them because the British High Commission makes us a small grant towards their upkeep. But we're short-handed, and the heavy monsoon rains don't help…"

The next day I am back at the cemetery, determined to make one more attempt at finding John Lang's grave. I am leaving for Delhi in a day or two, and it may be months, perhaps years, before I can return again.

This time I find the gate open. A small boy with little on goes skipping over the graves, like some mischievous cupid trying to resurrect dead lovers. His father, the *mali*, appears from behind a placid buffalo and gives me an elaborate salaam. Apparently Miss Garlah has already sent word of my coming.

The *mali* apologises for the condition of some of the graves near his outhouse. His buffalo is tethered to a crumbling obelisk. A cow and calf are tied to a slanting stone cross. Several graves are half-buried under straw and offal. Others appear to have vanished into a small ploughed field which now contains mustard. The strangest sight of all is a memorial tablet, commemorating a certain Captain Jones of her Majesty's 30th Foot, which lies flat on the steps of the *mali's* shack and provides an ideal platform for the gardener's tall and ornate hookah pipe.

The chances of finding John Lang's grave in this tumbled, crumbling heap now seem remote. But the *mali* offers to help me in my search and he is so anxious to please that I am loath to disappoint him. He starts scraping the mud off partly-obscured inscriptions and tells his small son, a merry little fellow with bright eyes and a disarming smile, to do the same. It is a glorious day, but the wind is from behind the *mali's* house, and there is no escape from the odour of sour milk and cow dung. I came in search of the dead, only to find the living.

We find several graves dating from 1864 and earlier, but John Lang's is not one of them. I begin to harbour mean thoughts about his wife. If she could disappear so suddenly and mysteriously with his manuscripts, it is unlikely that she would have bothered to give him an expensive and permanent grave.

"There were a few on this northern slope, sahib," says the *mali* after some time, "but we had a landslide a few years ago and the graves went down the *khud*."

This is enough to make me give up all hope. For all I know, John Lang's remains may well be at the foot of the mountain. My search becomes desultory, and I find myself muttering, "What does it matter, anyway? If a writer's any good, his books will be his monument. What need have we of tombstones to commemorate our passage on earth?"

But all the same I am disappointed. And seeing my disappointment, the *mali* makes renewed efforts to clean up some of the graves near the cattle shed. He cannot understand my whim, or anyone's sentimentality over old graves but he has warmed towards me, wants to please me, and would be quite willing to chisel "John Lang, died 1864" into any grave I choose, if it will make me happy.

Three weeks after leaving Mussoorie, I receive a letter from Miss Garlah, informing me that the old register had turned up and that John Lang had indeed been buried in the Mussoorie cemetery, on "C" terrace. On a subsequent visit I make my way to the spot and find the grave quite easily, under a thin covering of moss and ferns; but I'd had more fun on my earlier, rather muddled search.

"Familiar in their Mouths as HOUSEHOLD WORDS."
– Shakespeare.

Household Words

A WEEKLY JOURNAL CONDUCTED BY CHARLES DICKENS

This was a magazine brought out by Charles Dickens in the 1850s; the extract published here was written by an Australian, John Lang, himself a resident of Mussoorie for many years. It is being reproduced for the very first time since its original publication.

The Himalaya Club

It is some eighteen years since this institution was founded, at Mussoorie, one of the chief sanitaria in the Himalaya Mountains. Here all those who can obtain leave, and who can afford the additional expense, repair to escape the hot weather of the plains. The season begins about the end of April, and ends about the first week in October. The club is open to the members of the civil and military services, to the members of the bar, the clergy, and to such other private gentlemen who are on the government-house list, which signifies "in society." The club house is neither an expensive nor an elegant edifice, but it answers the purposes required of it. It has two large rooms, one on the ground floor, and the other on the upper story. The lower room, which is some sixty feet long by twenty-five wide, is the dining-room, breakfast-room, and reception-room. The upper room is the reading and the ball-room. The club has also its billiard-room, which is built on the ledge of a precipice; and its stables, which would astonish most persons in Europe. No horses, except those educated in India, would crawl into these holes cut out of the earth and rock.

Facing the side-door is a platform about forty yards long by fifteen feet wide; and, from it, on a clear day the eye commands one of the grandest scenes in the known world. In the distance are plainly visible the eternal snows; at your feet are a number of hills, covered with trees of luxuriant foliage. Amongst them is the rhododendron, which grows to an immense height and size, and is, when in bloom, literally covered with flowers. On every hill, on a level with the club, and within a mile of it, a house is to be seen, to which access would seem impossible. These houses are, for the most part, whitened without as well as within; and nothing can exceed in prettiness their aspect as they shine in the sun.

From the back of the club-house – from your bedroom windows (there are twenty-three sets of apartments) you have a view of Deyrah Dhoon. It appears about a mile off. It is seven miles distant. The plains that lie outstretched below the Simplon bear, in point of extent and beauty, to the Indian scene, nothing like the proportion which the comparatively pigmy Mont Blanc bears to the Dewalgiri. From an elevation of about seven thousand feet the eye embraces a plain containing millions of acres, intersected by broad streams to the left, and inclosed by a low belt of hills, called the Pass. The Dhoon, in various parts, is dotted with clumps of jungle, abounding with tigers, pheasants, and every species of game. In the broad tributaries to the Ganges and the Jumma, may be caught (with a fly) the mahseer, the leviathan salmon. Beyond the Pass of which I have spoken, you see the plains of Hindoostan. While you are wrapped in a great coat, and are shivering with the cold, you may see the heat, and the steam it occasions. With us on the hills, the thermometer is at forty-five: with those poor fellows over there, it is at ninety-two degrees. We can scarcely keep ourselves warm, for the wind comes from the snowy range; they cannot breathe, except beneath a punkah. That steam is, as the crow flies, not more than forty miles from us.

We are all idlers at Mussoorie. We are all sick, or supposed to be so; or we have leave on private affairs. Some of us are up here for a month between musters. We are in the good graces of our colonel, and our general – the general of our division, a very good old gentleman.

Let us go into the public room, and have breakfast; for it is half-past nine o'clock, and the bell has rung. There are not more than half-a-dozen at the table. These are the early risers who walk or ride round the Camel's Back every morning: the Camel's Back being a huge mountain, encircled about its middle by a good road. The majority of the club's members is asleep, and will defer breakfast until tiffin time – half past two. At that hour the gathering will be great. How these early risers eat to be sure! There is the major, who, if you believe him, has every complaint mentioned in Graham's Domestic Medicine, has just devoured two thighs (grilled) of a turkey, and is now asking Captain Blossom's opinion of the Irish stew, while he is cutting into a pigeon-pie.

Let us now while away the morning. Let us call on some of the grass widows. There are lots of them here, civil and military. Let us go first to Mrs. Merrydale, the wife of our old friend Charley, of the two hundredth and tenth regiment. Poor fellow! He could not get leave, and the doctors said another hot summer in the plains would be the death of his wife. They are seven hundred pounds in debt to the Agra bank, and are hard put to it to live and pay the monthly installments of interest. Charley is only a lieutenant. What terrible infants are these little Merrydales! There is Lieutenant Maxwell's pony under the trees, and if these children had not shouted out "Mamma! Mamma! Here is Captain Wall, Sahib!" I should have been informed that Mrs. Merrydale was not at home, or was poorly, which I should have believed implicitly. (Maxwell, when a young ensign, was once engaged to be married to Julia Dacey, now Mrs. Merrydale, but her parents would not hear of it, for some reason or other.) As it is, we must be admitted. We will not stay long. Mrs. Merrydale is writing to her husband. Grass widows in the hills are always writing to their husbands, when you drop in upon them, and your presence is not actually delighted in. How beautiful she looks! now that the mountain breezes have chased from her cheeks the pallor which lately clung to them in the plains; and the fresh air has imparted to her spirits an elasticity, in lieu of that languor by which she was oppressed a fortnight ago.

Let us now go to Mrs. Hastings. She is the wife of a civilian, who has a salary of fifteen hundred rupees (one hundred and fifty pounds) per mensem, and who is a man of fortune, independent of his pay. Mrs Hastings has the best house in Mussoorie. She is surrounded by servants. She has no less than three Arab horses to ride. She is a great prude – is Mrs. Hastings. She has no patience with married women who flirt. She thinks that the dogma –

"When lovely women go astray.

Their stars are more in fault than they" – is all nonsense. Mrs. Hastings has been a remarkably fine woman; she is now five-and-thirty, and still good-looking, though disposed to embonpoint. She wearies one with her discourses on the duties of a wife. That simpering cornet, Stammersleigh, is announced, and we may bid her good morning.

The average rent for a furnished house is about five hundred rupees (fifty pounds) for the six months. Every house has its name. Yonder are Cocky Hall, Bel-videre, Phoenix Lodge, the Cliffs, the Crags, the Vale, the Eagle's Nest, &c. The value of these properties ranges from five hundred to fifteen hundred pounds. The furniture is of the very plainest description, with one or two exceptions, and is manufactured chiefly at Bareilly, and carried here on men's shoulders, the entire distance – ninety miles.

Where shall we go now, for it wants an hour to tiffin-time? Oh! Here comes a *janpan*! (a sort of sedan-chair carried by four hill-men, dressed in loose black clothes turned up with red, yellow, blue, green, or whatever colour the proprietor likes best.) And in the *janpan* sits a lady: – Mrs. Apsley, a very pretty, good-tempered, and well-bred little woman. She is the grand-daughter of an English peer, and is very fond of quoting her aunts and her uncles."My aunt Lady Mary Culnerson," "my aunt the Countess of Tweedleford," "my uncle, Lord Charles Banbury Cross, &c." But that is her only weakness, I believe; and, perhaps, it is ungenerous to allude to it. Her husband is in the Dragoons.

"Well, Mrs. Apsley, whither art thou going? To pay visits?"

"No. I am going to Mrs. Ludlam's to buy a new bonnet, and not before I want one you will say."

"May I accompany you?"

"Yes, and assist me in making a choice."

There is not a cloud to be seen. The air is soft and balmy. The wild flowers are in full bloom, and the butterfly is on the wing. The grasshopper is singing his ceaseless song, and the bees are humming a chorus thereto.

We are now at Mrs. Ludlam's. The *janpan* is placed upon the ground, and I assist Mrs. Apsley to step from it.

Mrs. Ludlam is the milliner and dressmaker of Upper India, and imports all her wares direct from London and Paris. Everybody in this part of the world knows Mrs. Ludlam, and everybody likes her. She has by industry, honesty of purpose, and economy, amassed a little fortune; and has brought up a large family in the most respectable and unpretending style. Some people say that she sometimes can afford to sell a poor ensign's wife a bonnet, or a silk dress, at a price which hardly pays. What I have always admired in Mrs. Ludlam is that she never importunes her customers to buy her goods; nor does she puff their quality.

The bonnet is bought; likewise a neck-scarf for Jack. And we are now returning: Mrs. Apsley to her home, and I to the club. Mrs. Apsley invites me to dine with them; but that is impossible. It is public night, and I have two guests. One of them is Jack, who does not belong to the club, because Mary does not wish it.

Mrs Apsley says she wants some pickles, and we must go into Ford's shop to purchase them. Ford sells everything; and he is a wine, beer, and spirit merchant. You may get anything at Ford's – guns, pistols, swords, whips, hats, clothes, tea, sugar, tobacco. What is this which Ford puts into my hand? A raffle paper! "To be raffled for, a single-barrelled rifle, by Purdy. The property of a gentleman hard-up for money, and in great difficulties. Twenty-five chances at one gold mohur (one pound twelve shillings) each."

"Yes, put my name down for a chance, Ford."

"And Captain Apsley's, please." says the lady.

After promising Mrs. Apsley, most faithfully, that I will not keep Jack later than half-past twelve, and taking another look into those sweet eyes of hers, I gallop away as fast as the pony can carry me. I am late; there is scarcely a vacant place at the long table. We have no private tables. The same board shelters the nether limbs of all of us. We are all intimate friends, and know exactly each other's circumstances. What a clatter of knives and forks! And what a lively conversation! It alludes, chiefly, to the doings of the past night. Almost every other man has a nickname. To account for many of them would indeed be a difficult, if not a hopeless task.

"Dickey Brown! Glass of beer?"

"I am your man," responds Major George, N.I. Fencibles.

At the other end of the table you hear the word, "Shiney!" shouted out, and responded to by Lieutenant Fenwick of the Horse Artillery.

"Billy! Sherry?"

Adolphus Bruce of the Lancers lifts his glass with immense alacrity.

It is a curious characteristic of Indian society that very little outward respect is in private shown to seniority. I once heard an ensign of twenty years of age address a civilian of sixty, in the following terms: "Now then, old moonsiff, pass that claret, please."

The tiffin over, a *gool*, or lighted ball of charcoal, is passed round the table in a silver augdan (fire-holder). Every man present lights a cigar, and in a few minutes there is a general move. Some retire to the billiard-room, others cluster round the fire-place; others pace the platform; and two sets go upstairs into the reading-room to have a quiet rubber – from three till five. Those four men seated at the table near the window have the reputation of being the best players in India. The four at the other table know very little of the game of whist. Mark the difference! The one set never speak, except when the cards are being dealt. The other set are finding fault with one another during the progress of the hand. The good players are playing high. Gold mohur points – five gold mohurs on the rub – give and take five to two after the first game. And sometimes, at game and game, they bet an extra five. Tellwell and Long, who are playing against Bean and Fickle, have just lost a bumper – twenty-seven gold mohurs – a matter of forty-three pounds four shillings.

In the billiard-room, there is a match going on between four officers who are famed for their skill, judgment, and execution. Heavy bets are pending. How cautiously and how well they play! No wonder, when we consider the number of hours they practice, and that they play every day of their lives. That tall man now about to strike makes revenue out of billiards. I shall be greatly mistaken if that man does not come to grief some day. He preys upon every youngster in the native infantry. His name is Tom Locke. He has scored every station he goes to with his regiment. He is a captain in forty-seven off the red ball. His confederate, Bunyan, knows full well that luck has little to do with his success. He, too will come to grief before long. Your clever villains are invariably tripped of their commissions and positions in society.

It is five o'clock. Some thirty horses and as many ponies are saddled and bridled, and led up and down in the vicinity of the club. Everybody will be on the Mall presently. The Mall is a part of the road round the Camel's Back. It is a level of about half a mile long and twelve feet broad. A slight fence stands between the riders and a deep *khud* (precipice). To gallop along this road is nothing when you are accustomed to it; but, at first, it makes one very nervous even to witness it. Serious and fatal accidents have happened; but, considering all things, they have been far fewer than might have been expected.

The Mall is crowded. Ladies and gentlemen on horseback, and ladies in *jampans* – the *jampanes* dressed in every variety of livery. Men in the French grey-coats, trimmed with white serge, are carrying Mrs. Hastings. Men in the brown clothes, trimmed with yellow serge, are carrying Mrs. Merrydale. Jack Apsley's wife is mounted on her husband's second charger. "Come along, Captain Wall," she calls out to me, and goes off at a canter, which soon becomes a hard-gallop. I follow her, of course. Jack remains behind, to have a quiet chat with Mrs. Flower of his regiment; who thinks – and Jack agrees with her – that hard-riding on the Mall is a nuisance, and ought to be put a stop to. But, as we come back, we meet the hypocrite galloping with a Miss Pinkerton, a new importation, with whom – much to the amusement of his wife – he affects to be desperately in love. The Mall, by the way, is a great place for firtations.

Most steady-going people, like Mrs. Flower, not only think hard-riding on the Mall a nuisance, but make it the theme of letters to the editors of the papers, and sometimes will take the matter up, and write leading articles thereon, and pointedly allude to the fact – as did the late Sir C. J. Napier, in a general order – that beggars on horseback usually ride in the opposite direction to heaven. But these letters and leaders rarely have the desired effect; for what can a man do when a pretty woman like Mrs. Apsley says, "Come along – let us have a gallop"?

Why are there so very many people on the Mall this evening? A few evenings ago it was proposed at the club, that a band should play twice a week. A paper was sent round at once, and every one subscribed a sum in accordance with his means. Next morning the required number of musicians was hunted up and engaged. Two cornets, two flutes, two violins, a clarionet, a fife, and several drums. It is the twenty-ninth of May – a day always celebrated in "this great military camp," as Lord Ellenborough described British India. At a given signal, the band strikes up God Save the Queen. We all flock round the band, which has taken up a position on a rock beetling over the road. The male portions of us raise our hats and remain uncovered while the anthem is played. We are thousands of miles distant from our fatherland and our Queen; but our hearts are as true and as loyal as though she were in the midst of us.

This is the first time that the Himalaya mountains have listened to the joyous sound of music. We have danced to music within doors; but never, until this day, have we heard a band in the open air in the Himalaya mountains. How wonderful is the effect! From valley to valley echo carries the sound, until at last it seems as though

Every mountain now had found a band.

Long after the strain has ceased we can hear it penetrating into and reverberating amidst regions which the foot of man has never yet trodden, and probably will never tread. The sun has gone down, but his light is still with us.

Back to the club! Dinner is served. We sit down, seventy-five of us. The fare is excellent, and the champagne has been iced in the hail which fell the other night, during a storm. Jack Apsley is on my right, and I have thrice begged of him to remember that he must not stay later than half-past twelve; and he has thrice responded that Mary has given him an extension of leave until day-light. Jack and I were midshipmen together, some years ago, in a line-of-battle ship that went by the name of the House of Correction. And there is Wywell sitting opposite to us – Wywell who was in the frigate which belonged to our squadron – the squadron that went round the world, and buried the commodore, poor old Sir James! in Sydney churchyard. Fancy we three meeting again in the Himalaya mountains!

The cloth is removed, for the dinner is over. The president of the club – the gentleman who founded it – rises. He is a very little man of seventy years of age – fifty-three of which have been spent in India. He is far from feeble, and is in full possession of all his faculties. His voice is not loud; but it is very distinct and pierces the ear.

They do not sit long after dinner at the club. It is only nine, and the members are already diminishing. Some are off to the billiard-room, to smoke, drink brandy-and-water, and look on at the play. The whist parties are now at work, and seven men are engaged at brag. A few remain; and, drawing their chairs to the fire-place, form a ring and chat cosily.

Halloa! what is this? The club-house is heaving and pitching like a ship at anchor in a gale of wind. Some of us feel qualmish. It is a shock of an earthquake; and a very violent shock. It is now midnight. A thunderstorm is about to sweep over Mussoorie. Only look at that lurid forked lightning striking yonder hill, and listen to that thunder! While the storm lasts, the thunder will never for a second cease roaring; for, long before the sound of one peal has died away, it will be succeeded by another more awful. And now, look at the Dhoon! Those millions of acres are illuminated by incessant sheet lightning. How plainly we discern the trees and the streams in the Dhoon, and the outline of the pass which divides the Dhoon from the plains. What a glorious panorama! We can see the black clouds descending rapidly towards the Dhoon, and it is not until they near that level land that they discharge the heavy showers with which they are laden. What a luxury would this storm be to the inhabitants of the plains; but, it does not extend beyond the Dhoon. We shall hear the day after tomorrow that not a single drop of rain has fallen at Umbal-lah, Meerut, or Saharunpore.

The party from the billiard-room has come up to have supper, now that the storm is over. They are rather noisy; but the card players take no heed of them. They are too intent upon their play to be disturbed. Two or three of the brag party call for oyster-toast to be taken to the table, and they devour it savagely while the cards are dealt round, placing their lighted cheroots meanwhile on the edge of the table.

And now there is singing – comic and sentimental. Isle of Beauty is followed by the Steam Leg, the Steam Leg by the Queen of the May, the Queen of the May by the facetious version of George Bamwell, and so on. Jack Apsley – who has ascertained that dear Mary is quite safe, and not at all alarmed – is still here, and is now singing Rule Britannia with an energy and enthusiasm which are at once both pleasing and ridiculous to behold. He has been a soldier for upwards of sixteen years; but the sailor still predominates in his nature; while his similes have invariably reference to matters connected with ships and the sea. He told me just now, that when he first joined his regiment, he felt as much out of his element, as a live dolphin in a sentry-box, and he has just described his present colonel as a man who is as touchy as a boatswain's kitten. Apsley's Christian name is Francis, but he has always been called Jack, and always will.

It is now broad daylight, and high time for a man on sick-leave to be in bed. How seedy and disreputable we all look, in our evening dresses and patent-leather boots!

And observe this carnation in my button-hole – the gift of Mrs. Apsley – she gave it to me on the mall. The glare of the lights, and the atmosphere of smoke in which I have been sitting part of the night, have robbed it of its freshness, its bloom, and perfume. I am sorry to say it is an emblem of most of us.

Go home, Apsley! Go home, reeking of tobacco smoke and brandy-and-water – with your eyes like boiled gooseberries, your hair in frightful disorder – go home! You will probably meet upon the mall your three beautiful children, with their rosy faces all bloom, and their breath, when they press their glowing lips to those feverish cheeks of yours, will smell as incense and make you ashamed of yourself. Go home, Jack! I will tiff with you today at half-past two.

Two young gentlemen were victimised last night at the Brag party. The one, a lieutenant of the Foot Artillery, four thousand. The day after tomorrow, the first of the month, will be settling day. How are they to meet these debts of honour? They have nothing but their pay, and must borrow from the banks. That is easily managed. The money will be advanced to them on their own personal security, and that of two other officers in the service. They must also insure their lives. The premium and the interest, together, will make them forfeit fourteen per cent per annum on the sum advanced. The loan will be paid off in three years, by monthly installments. The paymaster will receive an order from the bank secretary to deduct for the bank so much per mensem from their pay. For the next three years they will have to live very mildly indeed.

There were also two victims (both youngsters) to billiards. One lost three thousand rupees in bets, another two thousand five hundred, by bad play. They, too, will have to fly for assistance to the banks. Captains Locke and Bunyan won, between them, last night, one thousand four hundred pounds. There was but little execution done at whist. Not more than one hundred and fifty pounds changed hands. Those four men who play regularly together, and who never exceed their usual bets, have very little difference between them at the end of each month – not thirty pounds, either way. This will not hurt them; for they have all good appointments, and have private property besides.

I find, on going to tiffin at Jack Apsley's, that Mrs. Jack has heard all about the winnings and losings at the club. Some man went home and told his wife, and she has told everybody whom she has seen. In a short time the news will travel to headquarters at Simlah, and out will come a general order on gambling, which general order will be read aloud at the Himalaya Club, with comments by the whole company – comments which will be received with shouts of laughter. Some youngster will put the general order into verse, and send it to a newspaper. This done, the general order will be converted into pipelights. This is no doubt very sad; but I have no time to moralise. My duty is simply to paint the picture.

Mrs. Apsley is not angry with her husband for staying up till daylight. She thinks a little dissipation does him good; and it is but a very little that Jack indulges in, for he is a good husband and a good father. Jack has a severe headache, but he won't confess it. He says he never touched the champagne, and only drank two glasses of brandy and water. But who ever did drink any more than two glasses of brandy and water? Jack came home with his pockets filled with almonds, raisins, prunes, nutcrackers, and two liqueur glasses; but how they got there he has not the slightest idea – but I have. Wywell, from a sideboard, was filling his pockets all the while he was singing Rule Britannia.

"Mrs. Apsley, I have some news for you." "What is it, Captain Wall?" "The club gives a ball on the seventh of June."

"You don't say so." "And what is more, a fancy ball."

The tiffin is brought in. Mulligatawny soup and rice, cold lamb and mint sauce, sherry and beer. The Apsleys are very hospitable people; but Mary, who rules the household, never exceeds her means for the sake of making a display.

The soup and a glass of wine set Jack up; and he becomes quite chirpy. He proposes that he and I and Wywell shall go to the fancy ball as middies, and that Mary shall appear as Black-eyed Susan. Then, darting off at a tangent, he asks me if I remember when we were lying off Mount Edgecombe, just before sailing for South America? But he requires a little more stimulant, for the tears are glistening in his soft blue eyes when he alludes to the death of poor Noel, a middy whom we buried in the ocean a few days before we got to Rio. In a very maudlin way he narrates to his wife the many excelled qualities of poor Noel. She listens with great attention; but, observing that his spontaneous emotion is the result of the two over-night glasses of brandy – plus what he cannot remember drinking over-night – she suggests that Jack shall make some sherry cobbler. What a jewel of a woman art thou, Mrs. Apsley! Several of the men who returned home, as Jack did, none the better for their potations, have been driven by their wives' reproaches to the club, where they are now drinking brandy and soda-water to excess; while here is your spouse as comfortable as a cricket on a hearth; and now that he confesses he was slightly screwed, you, with quiet tact, contradict his assertion.

For the next week the forthcoming fancy ball, to be given by the club, will be the chief topic of conversation amongst the visitors at Mussoorie. Mrs. Ludlam is in immense demand. She knows the character that each lady will appear in; but it is useless to attempt to extract from her the slightest particle of information on that head. This ball will be worth seven hundred and fifty rupees to Mrs. Ludlam.

Let us keep away from the club for a few days; for, after several officers have been victimised at play, their friends are apt to talk about the matter in an unpleasant manner. This frequently leads to a quarrel, which I dislike to witness.

Where shall we go? To the Dhoon. It is very hot there; but never mind. No great-coat, no fires, an hour hence; but the very lightest of garments and a punkah. The thermometer is at eighty- five degrees there. The Dhoon is not a healthy place in the summer. It must have been the bed of an enormous lake, or small inland sea. Its soil being alluvial will produce anything: every kind of fruit, European and tropical. You may gather a peach and a plantain out of the same garden. Some of the hedges in this part of the world are singularly beautiful, composed of white and red cluster roses and sweetbriars. There is an excellent hotel in the Dhoon, where we are sure to meet people whom we know.

Sure enough I find a party of five at the hotel; all club men and intimate friends of mine. They, too, have come down to avoid being present on the first setting day; for, if there should be any duelling, it is just possible that some of us might be asked to act as second.

We must dine off sucking-pig in the Dhoon. The residents at Mussoorie used to form their pig-parties in the Dhoon, just as the residents of London form their whitebait banquets at Greenwich. I once took a French gentleman, who was travelling in India, to one of these pig-parties, and he made a very humorous note of it in his book of travel, which he showed to me. Unlike most foreigners who travel in English dominions, he did not pick out and note down all the bad traits in our characters; but gave us credit for all those excellent points which his experience of mankind in general enabled him to observe.

The Governor-General's body-guard is quartered just now in the Dhoon, and there is a Goorka regiment here. The Dhoon will send some twenty couples to the fancy ball on the seventh. Every lady in the place has at this moment a Durzee (man tailor) employed in her back verandah, dressmaking. We are admitted to the confidence of Mrs. Plowville, who is going as Norma. And a very handsome Norma she will make; she being rather like Madame Grisi – and she knows it.

We return to the club on the second of June. There has been a serious dispute, and a duel has been fought; but happily, no blood shed. The intelligence of the gambling at the club has reached the Commander-in-Chief at Simlah; and he has ordered that the remainder of the leave granted to Captains Locke and Bunyan be cancelled, and that those officers forthwith join their respective regiments. The victims also have been similarly treated; yet every one of these remanded officers came up here on medical certificate.

It is the morning of the seventh of June. The stewards of the ball are here, there, and everywhere, making arrangements. Several old hands, who hate and detest balls, and who voted against this ball, are walking about the public room, protesting that it is the greatest folly they ever heard of. And in their disgust they blackball two candidates for admission who are to be balloted for on the tenth instant. They complain that they can get no tiffin, no dinner, no anything. But the stewards only laugh at them.

The supper has been supplied by Monsieur Emille, the French restaurateur, and a very splendid supper it is. It is laid out in the dining-room. Emille is a great artiste. He is not perhaps equal to Bragier – that great man whom Louis Philippe gave to his friend, Lord William Bentinck, when Lord William was going out to govern India – but Emille, nevertheless, would rank high even amongst the most skilful of cuisiniers, in Europe.

It is a quarter past nine, and we, of the club, are ready to receive our guests. The ladies come in *jampans*; their husbands following them, on horseback or on foot. It is a beautiful moonlight night. We are always obliged to wait upon the moon, when we give a ball in Mussoorie. Before ten o'clock the room is crowded. There are present one hundred and thirty-six gentlemen, and seventy-five ladies. Of the former nine-tenths are soldiers, the remainder are civilians. Of the latter, seventy are married; the remaining five are spinsters.

Here we all are in every variety of costume – Turks, Greeks, Romans, Bavarian – broom-girls, Medoras, Corsairs, Hamlets, Othellos, Tells, Charles the Seconds, and Quakers. Many have not come in fancy costume, but in their respective uniforms; and where do you see such a variety of uniforms as in an Indian ball-room? Where will you meet with so great a number of distinguished men? There is the old general: that empty sleeve tells a tale of the battle of Waterloo. Beside him is a general in the Company's service; one who has recently received the thanks of his country. He has seen seventy, but there is no man in the room who could, at this very time, endure so great an amount of mental or bodily fatigue. That youngster to the right of the general is to be made a brevet-major and a C.B. as soon as he gets his company. He is a hero, though a mere boy. That pale-faced civilian is a man of great ability, and possesses administrative talents of the very highest order. Seated on an ottoman, talking to Mrs. Hastings, is the famous Hawkins, of the Third Dragoons. Laughing, in the side doorway, is the renowned William Mumble. He is the beau ideal of a dashing soldier. Yonder is Major Starcross, whose gallantry in Afghanistan was the theme of admiration in Europe. And there is Colonel Bolt, of the Duke's Own. All of these men have been under very hot fire – the hottest that even Lord Hardinge could remember. All of them are decorated with medals and ribbons. Where will you see handsomer women than you frequently meet in a ball-room at Mussoorie, or Simlah? Amongst those now assembled there are three who, at any court in Europe, would be conspicuous for their personal attractions – Mrs. Merrydale, Mrs. Plowville, and Mrs. Banks. Mrs. Apsley is a pretty little woman; but the three to whom I have alluded are beautiful.

The dancing has commenced, and will continue until four o'clock, with an interval of half an hour at supper-time. The second supper – the ladies being gone – will then commence, and a very noisy party it will be. Unrestrained by the presence of the fair sex, the majority of those who remain will drink and smoke in earnest, and the chances are, there will be several rows. Ensign Jenks, when the brandy and water inflames him, will ask young Blackstone of the Civil Service, what he meant by coming up and talking to his partner during the last set of quadrilles. Blackstone will say, "The lady beckoned to him." Jenks will say, "It is a lie!" Blackstone will rise to assault Jenks. Two men will hold Blackstone down on his chair. The General will hear of this, for Captain Lovelass (who is himself almost inarticulate) has said to Jenks, "Cossider self unarrest!"

Jenks will have to join his regiment at Meerut, after receiving from the General a very severe reprimand.

While talking over the past ball, an archery meeting, or a picnic, is sure to be suggested. It must originate at the club: without the countenance of the club – which is very jealous of its prerogative – no amusement can possibly be successful. A lady, the wife of a civilian, who prided herself on her husband's lofty position, had once the temerity to try the experiment, and actually sent round a proposal-paper in her own handwriting, and by one of her own servants. She failed, of course. All the club people wrote the word "seen," opposite to their names; but withheld the important word "approved." Even the tradespeople at Mussoorie acknowledge the supremacy of the Himalaya Club.

The season is over. The cold weather has commenced in the plains. It is the fifth of October, and everybody at Mussoorie is on the move – going down the hill, as it is called. Every house which was lately full is now empty, and will remain so till the coming April. The only exceptions will be the schools for young ladies, and for little boys; the convent, the branch of the North West Bank, and Post Office. Invalided officers who reside at the Sanatarium during the summer, will go down the hill, and winter in Deyrah-Dhoon. In another month the mountains will be covered with snow; and it would be dangerous to walk out on these narrow roads; few of which are railed in.

Let us sum, up the events of the season: Four young men were victimised; two at cards and two at billiards. Two duels were fought on the day after the ball. In one of these duels an officer fell dead. In another the offending party grievously wounded his antagonist. Four commissions were sacrificed in consequence of these encounters. There were two elopements. Mrs. Merryclale went off with Lieutenant Maxwell, leaving her children under the care of the servants, until her husband came to take them away. Mrs. Hastings, who used to bore us about the duties of a wife, carried off that silly boy Stammersleigh. These elopements led to two actions in H. M. Supreme Court of Calcutta, and seven of us (four in one case and three in the other) had to leave our regiments, or appointments, and repair to the Supreme Court to give evidence. Some of us had to travel fourteen hundred miles in the month of May, the hottest month in India.

There was another very awkward circumstance connected with that season at Mussoori. The reader knows that Captains Locke and Bunyan were ordered to join their regiments, the unexpired portion of their leave having been cancelled by order of His Excellency the Commander-in-Chief. In the hurry of his departure from the hills, Locke had left in the drawer of a table a letter from Bunyan, containing a proposal to victimise a certain officer – then in Mussoorie – in the same manner that they had victimised one Lord George Straw, – namely, to get him to their rooms, and play at brag. Lord George Straw had lost to these worthies eighteen hundred pounds on one eventful night. The general opinion was, touching a very extraordinary fact connected with the play, that Lord George had been cheated. This letter from Bunyan to Locke was found by the servant of the officer who now occupied the apartments recently vacated by Locke. The servant handed it to his master, who fancying that it was one of his own letters, began abstractedly to read it. Very soon, however, he discovered his mistake. But he had read sufficient to warrant his reading the whole, and he did so. A meeting of gentlemen at the club was called; and, before long, Locke and Bunyan left the army by sentence of a general court-martial. I have since heard that Locke lost his ill-gotten gains in Ireland, and became eventually marker at a billiard-room; and that Bunyan, who also came to poverty, was seen driving a cab, for hire, in Oxford Street.

John Lang

A Mussoorie Miscellany

BY "THE RAMBLER" OF THE "MUSSOORIE TIMES'

WITH 18 ILLUSTRATIONS MAFASILITE PRESS
MUSSOORIE, INDIA

Written and published by H.C. Williams in the 1930s, this little booklet presents a lively account of murder, mayhem and assorted 'happenings' in Mussoorie. Some extracts are reproduced here. Williams was also the owner of a printing press and editor of a local newspaper called *The Mussoorie Times.*

A Mussoorie Miscellany

Lest the melancholy maid be robbed of her slumber after that wade through the mire of Mussoorie, the miscellany that follows is proferred as an unguent to her megrims. And what a heterogeneous medley to be sure. Blotches grave and splashes gay, ascents to the sublime and tumbles to the ridiculous, contributors and contributions of more than 100 years to the making of modern Mussoorie. How can one correctly catalogue so diverse a conglomeration? Therefore, as the writer gleaned them, so are they presented: the players and their performances, with no concatenation other than that each is a piece in the panorama of the past and passing Mussoorie.

And while some vital links with that past are still recognizable, such as the roads and dwellings named after the early settlers, these also will soon be submerged in the march of the maudlin, rechristenings, for who of the former generation would guess that Amawan Palace was once Hotel Cecil or that Padmani Niwas was Rushbrook?

There are other landmarks, how-ever, that will withstand the iconoclast yet a while, and for the generations still unborn will continue to flow the Hardy and Mussoorie's other falls, immortalizing earlier generations.

Why the "Hardy" Falls? Because when the boys of Mr. Macldock's school "discovered" the falls Mr. Hardy was Principal of the institution and had accompanied his charges on the ramble that led them to the spot. And lest the world not accept the students' christening, they laboriously carved the name in a rock by the fall and time has not effaced it.

But did you know that it was the same Hardy whose name is chalked on the door of a senior student's room in the earlier illustrated editions of Hughes' *Tom Brown's School Days?*

Perhaps even more appropriate, equally indelible, but far less dignified, was the christening of another Mussoorie water which had long evaded a suitable name. Picnicking by this water, on their own estate, the Hearsey family had as guest Mr. Moss of Himalaya Bank, affectionately known as "Mossy" by his associates. Scrambling over some rocks the guest slipped and fell to anchor well mid-stream, to a chorus of guffaws, and thus supplied the long elusive name – Mossy Falls!

Others there were, born in humble Mussoorie, or indebted to its comparatively insignificant Maddock's School for initiation into the three Rs, who have written their names across far wider spheres – Wilcox, builder of the "greater Assouan dam" and C.M. Gregory who built Mussoorie's Hotel Cecil and the row of shops to the east of the Library in 1905. And to whom do many of India's largest railway bridges owe their construction.

Another humble beginning made here was by the present Col. Sir Henry Gidney as Assistant Surgeon when Sedborough was first a simple dispensary, then a hospital, and, poor thing, a mortuary.

Those were expensive days for adequate medical attention and more so for dental overhaul, so perhaps you will readily sympathise with the poor unfortunate who sadly needed such attention and as sadly lacked the money to pay for it. He did have some land – a valuable site on which still stands one of Mussoorie's big amusement houses – and this he exchanged for the possession of a set of artificial teeth.

Even that agony could have been as nothing, however, to what one father had to endure for the unruliness of his sons. Self-appointed monarchs of all they surveyed, they made so regular a habit of acquiring what they wanted from shops in the Landour bazaar that the father had eventually to keep a cash deposit, constantly replenished, of Rs 250 with the civil authorities to balance the shopkeepers' monthly losses. No wonder then, that one of the sons came to a tragic end when shot dead in the Rajpore bazaar along with a gang of dacoits.

Exploits as wild, if less notorious, seemed almost common practice then of boys who will be boys as demonstrated by some lads of the Mussoorie School who raided the armoury, collected a small arsenal, and merrily tripped out to Kalimati (Rajpore) on *shikar*. Once there, they crossed a dry waterbed without difficulty, and then were trapped by a heavy downpour which flooded the stream. The Police and Forest Department subordinates, disguised as *shikaris* lest they scared their quarry into scurrying junglewards, eventually rescued the truants. A short spell of Coventry by confinement to the dormitory followed and there it was they finally secured their *shikar*. The windows overlooked the Principal's back yard and with various stratagems diabolically devolved, they were at last able to cook the Principal's goose. After much persuasion the bird was beguiled into accepting a tempting morsel offered on hook and line, was hauled aloft, and roasted in the fireplace. Was ever flesh more luscious or Coventry more kind?

Through the ages dormitory windows have lent themselves to adventurers' exploits and this mute cooperation still persists, as witness the painful undertaking in 1933, of an heroic parachutist in a local school who swathed himself in sheets for his baptismal practice and stepped into the air – but the air was not there. His sheets refused to "fill", and the damage was only varicoloured bruises and a deeply indented bed of colourful nasturtiums.

But all these bold, bad deeds by the boys pale before the sack of "Monte Christo" by the S. quartette. A true tale of the period when knights were bold, it began when one of the irresponsible quartette would have taken to wife the daughter of the master of Monte Christo. The irate father's adamant refusal brought the house down metaphorically and literally. On the night of the metaphorical collapse the families dined out leaving their domains invitingly open to the literal translators. The quartette marched in unchallenged, heaped the furniture and furnishings in the drawing room and set the pile alight. To repeat history as accurately as possible they left for the rescuers to read a lying placard on the porch "The Burning of Monte Christo by Titus".

A tale of revenge even more berserk, in the same connexion of man with maid, comes from the bazaar area and would be difficult to outdo in cunning. The villain of the piece was a tinsmith whose tinning all day left his pretty wife many hours for her own machinations which, in all truth, were innocent enough. The husband, however, doubted this possibility and in the time-honoured Indian method chopped off her nose. But that is a cognizable offence, and ever painstaking for perfection, he rounded off his devilry by assuming inebriation during this nocturnal performance and sober horror the next morning. Abject apology was offered and accepted; medical attention and silence was liberally paid for by the offender; love apparently resumed the reins of the household; and assured that no man would now accept his wife's overtures, the husband returned unperturbed to his tinning. Some months elapsed and then he showed the vileness of his scheme: he divorced the victim, thus ridding himself of what he believed was a faithless spouse, the while damning all hope of her finding another mate, himself evading the chastisement that was his due.

But witness the vagaries of human nature and weigh if you can the measure of sympathy or condemnation that is the portion of the next couple. As in the previous case, a young and pretty wife had daily to be left for hours while the husband attended his clerical duties at office. Being an almost wise man he realized the possible dangers of congested tenements, but lacking real wisdom distrusted his wife sufficiently to lock her in a single room that constituted their Mussoorie seasonal home. A flame of folly tinged with a spark of wisdom then burst forth again, and after locking the door on the outside he daily slipped the key under the door to his prisoner, lest fire or other catastrophe absolutely necessitated liberation in his absence. Returning home, a call at the door would warn the prisoner that it was time to pass the key back to her lord and master to enable his entry. And so the months sped by happily, he content that he had excluded the serpent from his Eden, and she jubilant at easy access to the forbidden. With mechanical regularity, excluding office holidays, the spoiler came. Eve reversed the order in her partner's game; admitted, wooed, and shooed her lover by the clock; and as the servile chattel of her legal lord gloried in his generous approbation, till Nemesis knocked in the guise of a simple ailment to her husband. Try as he would to control it his middle started ominous rumblings soon after his arrival at office and simply would not be silenced, eventually driving him home three hours earlier than usual. His knocking was unanswered for a while, and with each fleeting second the more rapidly he danced and the tighter griped his middle. At last the key tinkled under the door and the moment of his entry was the moment of forgetting even why he had come home. Even before he caught sight of his cowering wife he saw the base of the eternal triangle. For a moment the rivals gazed at each other in the deepest silence any of the trio present had ever known, before the husband forced his voice to the uttering of a single, common place sentence: *acha aap jaye* (Very well, you please go).

As though he had always contemplated such a situation and had long since determined just how to meet it, with perfect control the husband went back to his office, obtained a day's urgent leave of absence, and returning to his wife instructed her to pack for a journey. After ascertaining that she had taken all her personal belongings not excluding the tiniest, he bought her railway ticket to some distant destination, probably her maiden home, and almost before the train steamed out he turned his back on her – forever.

That this husband's fear of the possibility of a conflagration was not altogether unwarranted is supported by the fires that Mussoorie has experienced, of which the worst in the station's history was in the locality of the couple's residence, the Landour Bazaar. The blaze was too recent (May 5, 1935) to require more comment than that it had its compensating factor, for it was after that that the Municipal Board equipped itself with an extinguisher capable of dealing with large fires, or so it is hoped, for till now there has been no cause to test the appliance locally – nor is one wanted. A little surprising, is it not, that it took more than a hundred years of the town's existence before such a necessary safeguard was acquired? In that period one of the earliest fires destroyed the original "Phoenix Lodge" while it was yet a thatched building. The fire was caused by a smoke balloon released at an Indian wedding, which fell on the roof and set it alight.

In passing, it is worth recording that one of the latest replacements of thatched roofs by corrugated metal was that of "Powys Cottage", while there is still one European residence in the station that adheres to the old fashion: "Mary Ville" in Barlowganj.

Thou Shalt Not Kill

Many of these cases that follow were given wide publicity soon after their occurrence so that secrecy now about the perpetrators or victims appears unnecessary. Silence has been preserved only where it was considered essential. Deeper silence, by complete omission, of some cases has been resorted to where it was thought that publication even now might injure certain connections.

It is well that the first of these tragedies here recorded occurred as long ago as the early '40s. With publicity what it is today, a similar occurrence might so shock India as to relegate Mussoorie even further back than the position it has fallen to in recent years.

The seed was sown way down in the famous Chandni Chowk of Delhi. Mahabir had quarelled with his brother, Sohan, and not only severed partnership in the cloth store they possessed but had so severely thrashed the cause of the trouble, Sohan's wife, that with the young couple's expected son and heir still unborn, she died; just long enough after the quarrel, however, to secure Mahabir freedom from the punishment that was his due. Ostracised by those who "knew", Mahabir left Delhi permanently for Landour bazaar where business was brisk with less competition than the Delhi Chowk offered, and in increasing prosperity Mahabir forgot his troubles, and his brother.

Sohan apparently nursed his misfortune, for though the criminal was undiscovered, many made a shrewd guess as to who it was, particularly as just at the period of the crime we are reviewing, Sohan disappeared from the face of the earth, for he was never officially found. Mahibir was discovered by his neighbours in Landour bazaar one morning hanging, in company with the whole of his family, from the beams of his roof not far from Mullingar, all stone dead.

Also from Landour bazaar comes the sad case of "Raja" Elahie. It was Mr. Elahie's prosperity, gradually built upon the returns of a flourishing store of general merchandise that earned him the title of "Raja" amongst his associates. With increasing age Raja Elahie depended more and more on his employees to conduct his business, till wanting to launch a new venture he examined his finances and was stunned to find that he was, in reality, almost a poor man, robbed of his income by those he had most trusted. The shock was more than he could bear so he resorted to suicide, by poison.

One of the most futile and foolish of these tragedies was enacted on the lower slopes at the southern side of the same bazaar, by a constable who revenged requited love by shooting the plaything of his leisure (and possibly duty) hours. Foolish and futile because the man had several years of creditable service in the Force, and the damsel was only a butterfly whose ilk our "munshi" school used to aesthetically describe as "female brethren of the bazaar"! The heart-broken Romeo first strove to evade justice by bolting down the valley of the burning ghat and following the stream to the plains, but near Rajpore himself stopped his marathon. Faced with capture and still armed with his service rifle, he refrained, for some reason, from attempting a duel and was taken quite quietly. The "female brother" lies buried amongst her associates where she fell, lived and loved – not Bobby but his bobs.

Even more foolish almost was what young P. did on 1 August 1917, for in the same insane game he shot, not the cause of his flouted affection, but himself. Not, mind you, that the killing of her would have been any more justified than his own suicide. Is it not incredible what a ridiculously high value some appear to place on faithless love?! Well, well, young P. imagined he was in love with someone whose riper years should have been a deterrent to such hallucination, and when he found his outpourings wasted, he sought oblivion through the unpleasant slush of suicide. And what slush! – some have it that one held the suicide's scalp over the balcony of his abode, inviting passers-by to "see what he had done to himself".

Another suicide was enacted some years later in pathetic circumstances at Landour – to terminate the agonies of cancer. The victim, a gentleman of exceptional charm, begged his personal servant again and again to assist him to a more speedy death but his request was ignored. Then opportunity came when the house was deserted by all except the patient. Without delay or any ado he secured a loaded gun, held it between his knees with the muzzle pressed to his palate, and pulled the trigger to end his earthly suffering in a flash. God forgive him.

We next see, or rather should have seen years earlier (for these cases are not dealt with strictly chronologically), the case of G.H. yet another unfortunate suicide. A master of one of the Mussoorie schools, he seemed content enough and there appeared no reason for the drastic course he took, yet his colleagues were shocked to find his body, on 7 January 1898, way down one of the *khuds* near the school. Beside it lay a revolver, which, however, had not been used, death taking him by opium poisoning. The reader will notice that the tragedy occurred during the winter when the Mussoorie schools are closed for the long vacation, so one cannot believe that school activities played any part in the urge to take the step he chose.

There have been other somewhat similar tragedies in the history of the station, and in the years to come others must follow, for the agony of suffering is no less because of being borne in the health and holiday resort of Mussoorie.

The next tragic episode also concerns a master in one of our schools, and his wife, and is an example of what awful results can mature from petty inconsideration. Mrs. F. the wife of the school master, got herself inextricably enmeshed in a puerile defamation law suit each hearing of which was more distasteful to Mr. F. than the previous one, till the awful business drove him to a terrible solution. On the night of 24 November 1917, he armed himself with a loaded revolver, moved to his wife's bedside, and, finding her lying on her side in sound sleep, shot her through the back of the head. For no accountable reason he put the weapon under her pillow – obviously no one could have mistaken such a death for suicide – and then completed his plan. Calmly going into the lavatory, three rooms beyond his wife's bedroom, he leaned over his loaded rifle and shot himself. All this because of the lack of a little fellow-feeling.

That year, 1917, was Mussoorie's worst in respect of such happenings, and August the worst month of the year. Beginning with the suicide recorded it finished with a brutal murder. In a certain house on the southern slopes of the station there lived two aged sisters who, rumour said, had some disagreement with a hawker. On the night of Moharrum of that year, 30 August, a man called at the house, and hidden in the shadows, made the inmates believe he was a Telegraph Department peon with a telegram for them. The instant Mrs. Jane Mathews (widow) opened the door she was violently attacked by the caller, either with a knife or other weapon with which he lacerated the poor woman's head. With no trace of the murderer, the victim's sister and some others concluded it was the hawker.

A few years later Mussoorie was startled one morning to find the chaukidar of Messrs. Smith Rodwell's Carrying Agency (now the Railway Out-agency) murdered in the very heart of town. His assassin also remains undetected, but those who knew of the nightly happenings in the room where the victim slept might well have made a fair guess at identifying the culprit. It was alleged that a gambling school was conducted nightly on the premises, and that the chaukidar was murdered for his winnings of that night which were considerable.

Most recent of the murders at Mussoorie was that of Mr. Prakash Chand Banerjee, Manager of Messrs. Srimandar Dass and Company, on the night of 6 October 1933, and was another crime with the robbery of cash as its initial motive. Here again the culprit was never detected.

The assassin, or probably assassins, apparently studied Mr. Banerjee's habits for some time before launching their attack. They learned that Mr. Banerjee invariably strolled towards Landour bazaar, or to the Bengali Library, after shutting the shop. That evening it is probable that they even watched him shutting the shop and followed him to his quarters in the Himalaya Club flats, for Mr. Banerjee had time only to say a few words to his servant when a stranger informed him that someone from the bazaar wanted to speak to him.

Mr Banerjee innocently followed the man who led him along the Oaks Road, then led or forced him down the *khud*side and murdered him, the body not being discovered till the next morning.

Examination revealed that the victim had been clubbed, also that there had been an attempt at strangulation and that he had been knifed in the neck with the pen-knife he himself always carried.

On the day of the crime about Rs. 2,000 of the firm's money was deposited in a bank and some change was withdrawn. It was conjectured that the assassins learnt of some such transaction, possibly reversing the order to believe that Rs. 2,000 was withdrawn. The single key which Mr. Banerjee carried, and which opened both the lock of the shop door and of the cash till, was found missing from the body, and that same night, after the murder, the till was burgled.

An amusing echo was furnished by a *dhoti* with a certain *dhobi* mark which was found beside the body. On police enquiry from all the *dhobis* in Dehradun, it was found that every single one of them used the identical mark for a particular client.

What was not officially recognised as murder but certainly very closely resembled it, was a tragedy which might easily have been averted but for the stupidity of a constable on point duty in the Landour bazaar in 1934. The rubber toy of a child playing on the road rolled off the highway and fell into a conservancy tank full of water. The child in trying to recover it over-balanced and fell in. Within a very short time a crowd collected at the spot and several of the watchers made an attempt to save the child, but the constable on duty resolutely refused to allow anyone to "interfere" till the *Kotwal* arrived. This was literate interpretation and implicit obedience of the order to "let no one touch anything on the scene of an accident or crime till a senior officer arrived", if ever there was, but at what expense! Naturally the child drowned and after such long immersion failed to respond to artificial respiration.

Acts of God

It is a pity that so much of this book should be given to the recording of tragedies and there might be many who will feel that such depressing tales could well have been omitted but one must remember that in large measure the histories of most nations, and of many towns, have been born in, and nurtured on, blood. That such ghastly tragedies have been enacted at Mussoorie which is not merely a "short, seasonal", health resort, but has always been essentially a holiday station, makes it almost imperative that the writer record the grave with the gay; that the happy holiday-maker be turned a while from his giddy round of revelry to reflect how often, just in our most exuberant indulgence of life, we are verily at the threshold of death; but especially to ponder on what trivialities some of these tragedies were based and how simply they could have been averted by the merest vestige of fellow-feeling.

Not all these tragedies were however thus founded, and many were pure "acts of God", and as such the more inexplicable, such as the many ghastly deaths by falls down *khuds* and other precipitous places. Amongst the earliest of these on record is the destruction of Major Blundell and his pony, who, almost within the first decade of Mussoorie's history as here chronicled, "fell at this spot (in Landour) and was dashed to atoms"; and also in Landour, the Private in the cameronians who "fell at this spot and was killed".

But how many, or rather how very few, who in the past half century have enjoyed the walk around Camel's Back and been romantically thrilled at their introduction to "Lovers' Leap" (now almost forgotten as such) have realised that the name shrouds the memory of a double tragedy?

Jubilant of the present, and immersed in happy dreams of their approaching union and the future, the lovers cantered along their favourite ride, a carolling *kastura* within a stone's-throw welcoming them. Barely had the madrigal begun when the bird flashed past the riders to the valley below, almost brushing the lady's pony in its flight. The animal shied violently and backed dangerously near the edge of the road before the gentlemen could dash beside it and grab the bridle, only to make his own pony restive, and in a trice the lovers and their mounts had hurtled down the *khud* - the lovers' leap - to Death.

Another memorable fatality of almost the same nature on the same road, ushered in a fatal sequence which came a few weeks later and might thus also be considered a double tragedy. On 17 August 1883, little 5-year old Alice Gertrude Rheinhold had gone for her usual ramble along the Camel's Back Road accompanied by her nurse. Near the old Band House Alice stopped to play, while Nanny sat on the bench that used to be there and passed the time with needlework, till she was startled into action by a frightened, childish scream, and turned just in time to see her little charge slip through the space - a rather wide one - between the road and the bottom rung of the railings. Herself shrieking, she raced to the child's aid but by then the little mite was lying in a battered, crumpled heap more than 100 feet below.

Mr. Shaw, for long a familiar figure at Mussoorie, was walking in the vicinity at the time, and rushing forward to investigate, was confronted by the nurse speechless, and almost insane with shock. Indeed, the distracted woman was almost driven mad by the haunting memory continuing for years afterwards. There the poor woman stood wringing her hands and gazing into the *khud*, this being almost the only indication Mr. Shaw was given of what had occurred. The drop was a double one and, though Mr. Shaw was a youth then, he still wonders how he ever scrambled straight down that precipice and retrieved the child's remains. Little

Alice's father never recovered from the shock but, thank god, had to suffer the void for no more than two months, when he too passed over, on 16 October, and now lies beside his little girl.

There have been several similar accidents, many of them fatal, in the history of the usually carefree station, but 1935 has been one of the most unfortunate years for such mishaps there being six during the season, of which two proved fatal. Beginning early in the season a European child was killed by a fall at Landour. Then, on 7 June, occurred one of the strangest of such fatalities, a family, all adults, were strolling along the Town Hall Road in broad daylight – about 11 o' clock forenoon – when one of the party, Miss Marjorie Kingham, suddenly slipped between the bottom wire that fenced the road and the edge of the cliff to fall about 40 feet to the Mall. About mid-way down the cliff is a fairly wide ledge on which children have often been seen scrambling for flowers, and Miss Kingham fell on to this on her feet. Apparently, however, the impact fractured her leg, and being thus robbed of support the unfortunate woman rolled to the road below. She died that afternoon.

Three months later, almost at the same spot, a little child suffered a similar accident, but is, amazingly, alive to tell the tale. Between these two occurrences another little child rolled off a precipice near the Isolation Hospital and fell more than 20 feet into a concrete drain. He too now thrills at the experience. There followed another wonderful escape, when a man in Landour bazaar while cleaning out the guttering was thrown to the road below, a drop of about 30 feet, and fared no worse than to injure one hand. The last one came at the end of the season when an elderly woman rolled off her bed in the verandah of her house in Grant Lane. The unfortunate woman had already come to Mussoorie as an invalid for treatment. Her only injuries were bruises and considerable shock though the fall was about 20 feet.

Other accidents there have been almost more tragic, for, while definite responsibility for those cited above cannot really be laid at anyone's door, these that follow resulted from the deeds, purely accidental, of others than the victims, and thus evoke our deepest sympathy with the perpetrators, for, god knows, for them memory must have scotched the grandeur of life to nothingness.

Witness the shooting of Miss P. by her brother. The demented lad thought to rob recollection by fleeing from civilisation to the wooded khuds (below the family home) where he remained hidden for days! The poor lad had returned home from a Volunteer Rifle parade to find the family at breakfast. His sister noticing him armed with his rifle jokingly taunted him about indifferent gunmanship. Certain that his rifle was not loaded he replied by aiming at her, championing his marksmanship, and pressed the trigger – to admit the jester, Death.

In almost 'identical circumstances, on 5 November 1875, did young B kill his younger brother. Annually the victim's tomb is almost shrouded in red by the growth of an innocent weed, and because it has been found difficult to irradicate, the superstitious have woven their own tale around the phenomenon and tell of the "tomb that bleeds".

Beside a few minor motoring mishaps there have been two serious accidents on the Rajpore-Mussoorie motor road. There have, of course, been many more within the Rajpore and Dehra Dun limits. The first of the two occurred in the winter of 1930 when a gentleman from Dehra was driving an elderly relative uphill to view Mussoorie. At a spot between Kulukhet and Bhatta, the driver brought the car to a stop and alighted to investigate something in the engine, leaving his old relative in the closed car. Suddenly the vehicle started rolling down hill, backwards, upon which the young man shouted to his companion to jump out but before the poor old gentleman could even open the door the car leapt backwards over the cliff, taking its occupant with it, to be battered into matchwood and pulp 300 feet or more below. The car was absolutely new.

But what amazing escapes from death some have had in rickshaw accidents. One of the worst, way back in 1903, was for instance: a gentleman and his young son were being conveyed down Fitch's slope at a pace more fast than wise. The coolies lost control. As soon as the front pair realised that an accident was imminent, they jumped clear. The moment the gentleman saw this he believed he was facing death but had the presence of mind to throw his child out on the Mall and the next instant rickshaw and occupant had smashed through the railings to a drop of several feet, the rickshaw in splinters, and the gentleman unacquainted with death and no more than vilely shaken but more vilely angry.

The Municipal Board thoughtfully placarded this slope and others with the warning: "Dangerous – drive slowly", for passengers who still fly past to read with their hearts in their mouths or, perhaps, in each other's keeping.

A similar surprising escape was experienced by a gentleman and his son near Kincraig, in the summer of 1933. The vehicle was conveying them uphill from Sunny View when the outside wheel bumped off the edge of the road. Here too, some of the coolies promptly let their charge go, and it went, complete with its fares, rolling some distance backwards down the road till it tumbled off, a complete wreck. Bruises and much sympathy were the lot of the passengers.

Amongst these "acts of God" must be included the tragedies due to lightning. Of these we have seen what happened on Burnt Hill but there was an amazing sequel to what was already a sequence of such tragedies on that hill; that is, if we accept as correct what the oldest generation of Mussoorietes have said about the early victims of the Burnt Hill Catastrophe being relations of a Captain Spread similarly killed many years later. It means, in fact, that lightning followed the family to kill those of it who dared reside at Mussoorie!

Captain Charles Henry Deane Spread, of the Invalid Establishment, Landour, was struck by lightning and killed at Bala Hissar (the old red building) on 3 September 1879. He was preparing to develop some photographic plates and in a heavy shower was collecting rain water for the process from the guttering when he was struck dead.

On the same day 24 years later, 3 September 1903, Miss Eleanor Amy Nunn was similarly killed at The Abbey. She was a teacher. During a heavy shower of rain she was asked to close the door and she went to comply when lightning staick a tree in the compound, raced to the eaves and thence to her. Crumpling in a heap on the floor she was just able to ask to be left untouched before she expired.

Many years later the Bala Hissar building, not the identical one, however, where Captain Spread was killed, was again struck by lightning but there are some who question this and declare that a defective electric supply system wire was to blame. Whatever it be, the fact remains that Mr Mackintosh, then the Principal of Bala Hissar was at that time urged, much against his will, to go to a cinema show. He agreed reluctantly but thanked God for his eventual assent when he returned in a storm and found his room on fire. And yet once again did Bala Hissar suffer similarly, Mr Fitzpatrick being the suferer.

Then, of course there have been several cases of electrocution, fatal, or merely shocked, resulting from the electric supply system. The last of these fatalities occurred at Woodville early in the 1935 season. One of the most unusual, however, was in 1926 during the monsoon when a horse and rider were shocked on a canter along the Mall by an exposed "earth" wire which the animal trod on.

But fatalities from all these causes are far outweighed by that which repeatedly overtakes the unwary who seek the bracing climate of these hills and are sent to death, indirectly, by that climate. Hundreds have fled from the heat of the plains only to find that Mussoorie's cooling zephyrs are more generous than they had anticipated and inadequate provision against this drives them to the error of sleeping with a coal fire in a closed room, and to death or severe injury by asphyxiation.

Periodically these coal gas poisonings are reported in spite of dozens of similar mishaps. They are merely a result of ignorance and it is the illiterate who have suffered most by them, so it is earnestly hoped that readers of these lines will warn their servants and the unwary generally, of this danger.

In all Mussoorie's history there has been only one death in the station by that terrible affliction, hydrophobia. Thank God, there is little likelihood of there ever being another now that the Municipal Board has a seasonal anti-rabies centre to deal with infection, while at Dehra Dun there is a centre permanently open. The death was that of Lieutenant Fredrick St. George Tucker, of The Bengal Staff Corps, and occurred on September 28, 1885.

Who Owns the Dun!

Previous chroniclers dealing with the history of the Dun have taken for granted the annexation of the Dun by the British from the Gurkhas, overlooking the possibility that the Gurkhas did not own the Dun at the time of "annexation". From documents this writer has studied it appears that the Dun then belonged to, and still is, the property of a single Anglo Indian family.

As incredible as this might seem, the documents referred to tell of Raja Sudarshan Sah selling to Major Hyder Young Hearsey the *parganas* of Chandee (District Moradabad) and Dhoon for a sum of Rs. 3,005 by a deed dated 22 June 1811, duly signed and witnessed. The very next year Major Hearsey made a sale of Pargana Chandee, and part of the sale deed said:

...I have made over to the Government Officials the Imperial Firmans, together with the deed of sale, executed in my favour by Raja Soodarshan Sah. Although the Imperial Firmans are for both the Pargannas Dhoon and Chandee, yet I have only sold the Zamindarie and the rights and interests accruing thereon of the Parganna of Chandee. But I here promise that when the Parganna Dhoon shall come within the possessions of the Honourable East India Company, I will sell the villages belonging to it to the aforesaid Company. With this view I have written this deed etc...

The deed was witnessed by four European military officers and two Indians, and was signed on 28 October 1815, but stipulates that payment (for the Chandee pargana) shall be made as from 1 January 1812, and shall be Rs. 1,200 annually. "This sum to be made payable to me and my heirs and successors from generation to generation in perpetuity".

One of those successors is still (1935) being paid Rs. 100 per month, or Rs. 1,200 annually by the government, which would appear to be an acknowledgement of the legality of the document quoted. If the claim for this sum is legal, how does the rest of the claim (for the Dhoon pargana) become invalid?

Many earlier chroniclers of "memoirs" and memories of the Dun admit Major Hearsey's possession of such lands, and add that he sold those lands to the government. Was it the land, or merely part of it, as these documents appear to prove? Then again, supposing, as has been pointed out to the writer, that by the time the sale deed was executed (28 October 1815) the Gurkhas had overrun the Dun and had to be driven out by government troops, at great expense of life and money, thereby giving the government full possession, how does that annul the phrase in the document: "I here promise that when the Parganna Dhoon shall come within the possession of the Honourable East India Company I shall sell etc. etc..."? That phrase would seem to imply that both parties to the deed knew that others were in temporary possession of the Dun; that one of the parties to the deed (The H.E.I. Company) would eventually take over possession; and that when that happened the other party (Major Hearsey) would sell and, naturally, be paid for the property.

It is significant that this deed was signed on 28 October 1815, whereas the Gurkhas were driven from the Dun in 1814, and less than a month after the execution of the sale deed the government ordered the annexation of Dun - 17 Nov. 1815.

Does the Dun rightfully belong to the Hearsey family, or does it not?

The station is supposed to have derived its name from the former abundance on these hills of the shrub *Coriaria Nepalensis*, the vernacular name of which is *Mansur*, or *Mansuri*. The Europeans eventually dropped the "n". The station's position on the map is Latitude 30 27' 30" Longitude 78 6' 30"; the climate varies from 23°F to about 90°F, and the annual rainfall from 80" to 115". The snowfall varies considerably more. The actual year of the earliest and latest snowfalls have been forgotten, but the dates, respectively, are 11 November and 13 March, while in February 1814 snow lay on the ground for two days at Dehra Dun.

No one who visits the station can ever quite forget the view of the Dun and the plains beyond the Siwaliks, unsurpassed by the scenery of any other Indian hill resort.

During the rains the view is at its best and from several homes near Barlowganj it has been possible, with a pair of good binoculars, to follow the racing at Dehra Dun, while even the naked eye can pick out the Roorkee canal.

But would you believe that these innocent factors could cause anyone heartbreak? No? Well, you would have thought differently if you could you have asked one of the engineers who was deputed to supervise the construction of the less ambitious Eastern Canal of Dehra Dun. Of course, this was long after the early 1800s; with which the story begins.

To an ingenious engineer it was an easy matter to kill two birds with one missile, so when the *bara sahib* unexpectedly visited the construction works he found his subordinate not there, but diligently supervising construction through a pair of field glasses from Mussoorie!

There is sometimes a surprisingly wide difference between the climatic conditions of the low lying parts of the station and the peaks of Mussoorie, and if you would refrigerate yourself - you will need to after the climb - try these morning walks to Mussoorie's eminences:

* Peak above St. Peter's Church, Landour; 7,527 feet above sea level.
* Lal Tibba, Landour; 7,439 feet above sea level.
* Benog (West end); 7,433 feet above sea level.
* Blucher's Hill (West end); 7,20$ feet above sea level.
* The Abbey; 7,092 feet above sea level.
* Gun Hill (Camel's Back); 7,029 feet above sea level.
* Vincent Hill; 7,006Teet above sea level
* The Convent (Waverley); 6,985 feet above sea level.
* Observatory (Evelyn Hall); 6,872 feet above sea level.

If the Trojan finds such mild exercise insufficient to his needs he might strive to emulate a former day officer of the Survey Department, Mr. B. B. Osmaston, who left Deota at 4 a.m. and, having marched the whole way, dined at Dehra Dun that night 16 hours later, in which period he had covered only 90 miles! As you might gulp more salt than is pleasant after reading that perhaps it is wise to add that there are those at Mussoorie now who will gladly testify to the statement. Lt. Cadell of the same department was another of those mighty men who moved when they hiked.

But perhaps you prefer ingesting *chota bazri* on a pony, in which event you might try and improve on Mr. Scott's breakneck rides from Mussoorie down to Rajpore, which he did as regularly as clockwork within the half hour.

Royal Receptions and a Regal Farewell

In 1882, the Tivoli Garden on the Hearsey estate in Barlowganj was opened to the public. In passing, we find that Barlowganj was so named after Colonel (later General) Barlow, whose residence was Barlow Castle, now Whytbank – very much minus the "castle". Like most houses of the period, it too was originally a thatched bungalow know as Ravens' Wood. The estate was eventually sold by the Johnstone family to the Alliance Bank in 1928.

At that time there were 340 European residences in the station and 140 Indian. The separate individual residences, at this time were 1,406, of which 743 were in the civil area, 110 in the cantonment, and 553 in the bazaar area.

Probably the profits to the Municipal Board from hall rents sponsored the building of Mussoorie's first amusement house, the Rink, built by Mr. Joseph Miller who was sole proprietor till 1890. He then combined with a syndicate which in 1892 was made a private limited company possessing the "Mussoorie Skating Rink and Amusement Club Ltd." till 1898. That year Mr. C. Wilson became sole proprietor but the property subsequently came into the possession of the Bank of Upper India Limited. At the close of the War it was sold to the Mussoorie Development Company Limited, the present proprietors. During the War years Mr. Fitch leased the Rink from the Bank and it was then reputed to have returned the largest profits in its history.

This amusement centre enjoyed its most prosperous days before theatre in India was superseded by the talkies, but in spite of the greatly altered conditions, the Rink is still a vital force in the life of the station, and yearly an increasing number of visitors flock to it for roller skating, the Rink's chief offering now.

To Mussoorie 1883 sent another ex-Amir of Afghanistan, Yaqub Khan, in the escort of four men of the Northumberland Fusiliers (the 5th Foot) one of whom was Mr. J.C. Fisher who so thoughtfully "does" for us after we have finished doing all we want for – or to – ourselves.

This political prisoner was installed at "Believes" and had free access to all parts of the station and its surroundings and frequently took advantage of it, riding around on one or other of his many excellent ponies. But even he underestimated the extent of his freedom as the following incident illustrates.

Ex-Amir Yaqub Khan was invariably accompanied by a British Political Officer, who on the many rides around the station could never understand the prisoner's habit of suddenly spurring his pony into a fast gallop, without a word of warning to his companions. These bursts of speed became more and more frequent and the officer eventually put it down to mere whim, till one day the full meaning of it was borne to him in a most discomforting manner. The officer had stopped to converse with a friend while the rest of the cavalcade ambled on till a bifurcation of the road was reached, near the Library, whereupon the prisoner spurred hard for his pony to shoot forward down the road to Rajpore – and perhaps, to freedom. That, at least, was what the officer concluded the dash was maneuvered for, and his only chance of intercepting the run-away was to urge his own pony to leap down the steep drop to the road below, which is what he did. The Governer-General was informed of the incident by telegram and orders were sought in the event of further similarities. The reply was: "Don't hurt one hair of his head".

So we pass on to 1884, and in April 1884 we find Mussoorie being hurriedly tidied; brooms, paint, spit and polish everywhere, with the greatest bustle and expense centred in Tivoli Garden for the reception of the Duke and Duchess of Connaught, who arrived on 17 April for *shikar* followed by a memorable lunch and much merry-making in the present ruins, then palatial; in the present jungle, then Tivoli Garden.

The next step forward is a long one to 1901, and while it affected Mussoorie considerably it really stopped short at Dehra Dun. This was the extension and opening of the Hardwar-Dehra Dun Railway.

In March 1905 the station received its second overhaul in the history of a century and a quarter for the visit of Her Royal Highness, the Princess of Wales (Queen Mary), who stayed at the Charleville Hotel – the only hotel in India to be thus honoured. Her Royal Highness appeared to enjoy her stay, and amongst the souvenirs she took home with her were some of Mussoorie's famous walking sticks, purchased in Landour bazaar, at least one of which was probably given to the late King Edward VII, who possessed a large collection of walking sticks.

The great Indian earthquake of that year damaged many buildings in the station. Barlowganj suffered badly, and Tivoli Garden lost its pavilion and other structures. The effect of the tremor on the clock in the steeple of the Methodist Episcopal Church in Kulri urged a certain wit to burst into doggerel:

The Kulri clock has had a shock.
Enough to knock it off its block.
And make it rock – ah!
Hanhart and Bechtler both have tried
To titivate its shocked inside.
So now they've called Fisher
The watchmaker and undertaker!

Mr. Hanhart and Mr. Bechtler were both proprietors of jewellery and watch repairing establishments. Mr. Fisher's accomplishments the doggerel makes no secret of.

In 1908 the government bought the Castle Hill estate for the sum of Rs. 3,00,000 to accommodate the Survey of India Drawing Office, and field parties during recess. Few of the buildings on the estate are now used and, at a fair price, the government would probably be glad to sell the property.

One of Mussoorie's greatest blessings came to it on 24 May (Empire Day) 1909. On that evening, the electric lights were switched on. Mussoorie's hydroelectric scheme, incidentally, provides, or did provide till very recently, the highest lift of water in Asia and one of the highest lifts in the world – 1,700 feet. The Mussoorie City Board is the sole proprietor of the undertaking.

When the Board first supplied electricity to private dwellings the charge was Rs. 25 for each point installed, to be paid in installments over ten years. It was not until 1919 that dimming the lights, popularly known as "the wink", was resorted to. Since then, for all these years, the lights have "winked" nightly some time between four minutes to nine o'clock and three minutes past nine o'clock to let the public know it is exactly nine o'clock. It was not till 1934 that the authorities realized that this was an infringement of the Indian Electricity Act and had to obtain special sanction from the Government to continue it!

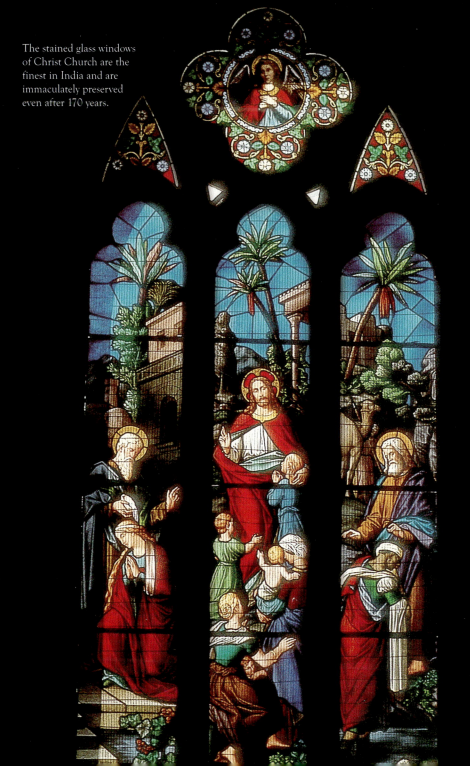

The stained glass windows of Christ Church are the finest in India and are immaculately preserved even after 170 years.

Shyan and Sunny were old-time residents of Happy Valley, till Sunny left us. The Plaisance is a cosy family-run hotel for those who are looking for a home away from home.

Arthur Fisher, a man for all seasons was a cinema-operator at Picture Palace (Mussoorie's first Electric Cinema). Later he became a helper to the undertaker of the cemetery, spending his lonesome last years in Miss Garlah's Woodland School.

The far-out world of Woodstock School provides an education with a difference to students from some 30 countries.

The monsoon light bathes the path to Lal Tibba in a mauvish glow.

Mont George should probably have been renamed Mont Abu – it's been home to Abu and Lakshmi Tripathi's family for more than three decades now.

Vinod is not unlike the protagonist in Arnold Bennett's Riceyman Steps, itching to sell. He lives amongst his acquired relics in what used to be the old Top Shop below the Clock Tower.

The late Princess Sita of Kapurthala with friends at Vermont, once the home to the Badhwar family. The ladies took turns at hosting tea and a bridge game during their sojourn in Mussoorie many summers ago.

The late Gen. Ram of the Nursing Services, the only Indian recipient of the Florence Nightingale Award, lived happily in her single room crowded with souvenirs of the past and her faith till she went away to meet her Maker.

St. George's College, the oldest boys' school in Mussoorie, straddles a spur off the main road near Barlowganj, overlooking the Doon Valley.

Facing page: The ruins of the old Bohle's Brewery in Barlowganj with the imposing Sikander Hall – home to generations of the Skinner family – in the background.

Wynberg Allen started out as an orphanage over 120 years ago. It occupies the site of the old Bala Hissar estate and has grown into one of the bigger schools in the district.

Ranjit Das once lived in the Landour Cemetery and frightened intruders away. Here he sits smoking his usual chillum under a strapping cypress planted in 1870 by H.H. the Duke of Edinburgh.

On the grounds of the old Charleville Hotel in Happy Valley lies the sprawling Lal Bahadur Shastri Academy of Administration, where for fifty years all the officers of the Indian Administrative Services have been given their initial training.

A view of the precipitous climb from the Landour bazaar to Lal Tibba.

A funeral in progress. Rev. R.C. Alter, retired as the Principal of Woodstock School, has (with Padre Das) read the funeral service for over 40 years in Mussoorie. The Camel's Back and Landour cemeteries have graves dating as far back as the 1830s. Among the most famous graves are those of F.E. Wilson ('Pahari Wilson'), the author John Lang, and a survivor of the Charge of the Light Brigade, Alfred Hindmarsh.

H.R.H. Rajmata Prithvi Bir Kaur of Jind used to sit at the piano playing "Ah, Sweet Mystery of Life", an old Nelson Eddy favourite. "Pretty" got her good looks from her Rumanian grandmother. Life has been rather dull since she went away to the Great Beyond.

Top: Mullingar decked out in festive streamers.

Bottom: Colonel Young's potato garden at the Mullingar has seen many incarnations. Presently it is home to many Bhotia families who came here from the border abutting Tibet.

Many of the Landour merchants are third-generation descendants of the businessmen who followed the British troops up to Landour in the 1830s. The narrow bazaar, never meant for modern vehicular traffic, is now something of a bottle-neck.

Top: The late Mr. Lord was appropriately named, for, as the undertaker of the Camel's Back Cemetery, he saw many to their graves.

Facing page: Publisher's prerogative! This picture of Ruskin Bond is being used simply because he hates it more than any other and the publisher wants to get even with him for delaying the delivery of the manuscript. Here Ruskin is training two roosters to sing like Domingo and Pavarotti. Of course these are not the only birds he likes!

Bottom: Gerald Powell was the last Powell to be living in Barlowganj, Mussoorie till he passed away in the U.K. His forefathers were among the pioneers of this town and Dehradun.

The late Jim Keelan was born in Mussoorie and never moved out. A talented water colourist, Keelan had an encyclopaedic memory of Mussoorie's past. His wife, Patricia, ran a free dispensary at Vincent Hill for the villagers for many years. Amongst his other achievements, Keelan once shot a marauding black bear on the slopes outside his cottage.

A winter evening vista from St Asaph Estate, near Lal Tibba, framed by icicles from the roof.

Char Dukan, literally just four shops, has its own bank, a post office and a cyber cafe too, catering to the material needs of the Landour residents. Its specialities are "bun-n-omelettes", cheese toasties, and recently, waffles!

"If they don't have it, you don't need it!" a customer was reported to have exclaimed to his wife at Prakash's store in Sister's Bazaar. Famed for its cheese, jams and chutneys – a boon for those who live here.

Library Chowk, now known as Gandhi Chowk, serves as a convenient public Square near the old band stand. The old Mussoorie library is well-preserved due to the efforts of the late Mrs. Maisie Gantzer. This is a Holi bonfire and not a book-burning!

"Howdy!" That's how Nandu Jauhar once greeted his friends. He was the affable owner of the Savoy Hotel and was known for his ready wit and warm hospitality. He reminded one of Bob Hope – but of course, Nandu was better looking!

Top: Vivid memories of the days of wine and roses echo in the Chateau, now home to Brigadier Sukhjit Singh, the present H.H. Maharaja of Kapurthala.

Bottom: Indian Administrative Services probationers learn to ride, continuing the tradition of the Mofussil Magistrate from the days of the Raj. Today's magistrate will of course ride around in a red-beaconed car.

Not long after the Dalai Lama and his followers came to Happy Valley (around 1960) the Tibetan refugee community built their own Buddhist temple, one of the more colourful and attractive places around Mussoorie.

A view of Banderpuch from Lal Tibba as winter cloaks everything in startling white.

Housed in the Kellogg Church (no relative of the breakfast cereals) over a hundred years old, the Language School offers excellent courses to students and wanderers from overseas in Urdu, Hindi, Hindustani and other languages.

Top: Re-afforestation involving school children has slowly brought back much of Mussoorie's green cover.

Bottom: Hampton Court gets its name from the estate where the school started. It is a convent school for small boys, where the author spent a "formative year" of his life.

Ron and Saroj Kapadia were popular figures on the Mussoorie hillside. Ron Kapadia has gone on to the happy hunting grounds and Saroj now lives on her own.

© Roli Books, 2010

Published in India by Roli Books Pvt Ltd
M-75 Greater Kailash II Market
New Delhi-110 048, India
Ph: ++91-11-4068 2000; Fax: ++91-11-2921 7185
E-mail: info@rolibooks.com, Website: www.rolibooks.com

ISBN: 978-81-7436-033-5

All rights are reserved. No part of this publication may be transmitted
or reproduced in any form or by any means without prior
permission from the publisher.

Concept and picture selection: Pramod Kapoor
Design and layout: Naresh L. Mondal
Production: Naresh Nigam and Jyoti Dey

Printed and bound in India

Photo Credits
For pictures other than those of Ganesh Saili
British Library: Pages 2-3, 8-9, 12-13, 18-19, 24, Panorama Gatefold
Pramod Kapoor: Pages 100, 108-109, 112-113, 126-27, 132-33, 138-39
Roli Collection: Gatefold (postcards)
Victor Banerjee: Page 122